DEATH AND DYING

The MIT Press Essential Knowledge Series

A complete list of the titles in this series appears at the back of this book.

DEATH AND DYING

NICOLE PIEMONTE AND SHAWN ABREU

The MIT Press | Cambridge, Massachusetts | London, England

The MIT Press would like to thank the anonymous peer reviewers who provided comments on drafts of this book. The generous work of academic experts is essential for establishing the authority and quality of our publications. We acknowledge with gratitude the contributions of these otherwise uncredited readers.

This book was set in Chaparral Pro by New Best-set Typesetters Ltd. Printed and bound in the United States of America.

Library of Congress Cataloging-in-Publication Data

Names: Piemonte, Nicole, author. | Abreu, Shawn, author.
Title: Death and dying / Nicole M. Piemonte and Shawn Abreu.
Other titles: MIT Press essential knowledge series.
Description: Cambridge, Massachusetts : The MIT Press, [2021] | Series:
    MIT Press essential knowledge series | Includes bibliographical references
    and index.
Identifiers: LCCN 2020027077 | ISBN 9780262542425 (paperback)
Subjects: MESH: Death | Attitude to Death | Right to Die | Hospice Care |
    Terminal Care
Classification: LCC BF789.D4 | NLM BF 789.D4 | DDC 155.9/37—dc23
LC record available at https://lccn.loc.gov/2020027077

10   9   8   7   6   5   4   3   2   1

To Joy and Ralph Piemonte, who went before us and taught us so much—
and to all of those who have shown us the fullness of life while facing its end.

CONTENTS

SERIES FOREWORD

The MIT Press Essential Knowledge series offers accessible, concise, beautifully produced pocket-size books on topics of current interest. Written by leading thinkers, the books in this series deliver expert overviews of subjects that range from the cultural and historical to the scientific and technical.

In today's era of instant information gratification, we have ready access to opinions, rationalizations, and superficial descriptions. Much harder to come by is the foundational knowledge that informs a principled understanding of the world. Essential Knowledge books fill that need. Synthesizing specialized subject matter for nonspecialists and engaging critical topics through fundamentals, each of these compact volumes offers readers a point of access to complex ideas.

Death is all around us. I mean this in the abstract sense, of course: death is inevitable and inescapable, an undeniable part of the human condition. But I also mean this in the personal sense: it's all around *us*—Shawn and me—who both work in medicine and see sickness and death all the time. Shawn is a doctor who practices hospice and palliative medicine, and I am a faculty member and assistant dean at a medical school as well as a researcher with a focus in medical humanities and end-of-life care—an academic career inevitably shaped by the experience of caring for my mother while she was dying of ovarian cancer when I was a young college student.

Because of our shared professional interests, Shawn and I have always known that we wanted to write about death and dying, seeing firsthand the ways that medicine and medical education can fall frighteningly short when it comes to helping our physicians learn to care well for patients at the end of life. What we didn't know, however, was that when we began writing this book, my father would be diagnosed with terminal cancer, and we'd watch him steadily diminish into a shadow of himself. After his diagnosis, we knew we wanted to help my dad live and die as well as he could and naively assumed we could help make this happen for him, given our shared "expertise."

What we quickly learned, though, is how easy it is to get caught up in the wheels of the medical system—a system we thought we knew how to navigate. The wheels of the health care machine are swift and nearly imperceptible—oiled by a series of decisions, some of them seemingly small and almost all of them benevolent—that move patients, families, and even clinicians to a place they never intended.

We also didn't know—and could never have anticipated—that just weeks after submitting a final draft of this book to our publisher, a viral pandemic would sweep the globe, rapidly transforming the way we live and the way we die. We are in the midst of the COVID-19 pandemic as we write these words, and we are still bearing witness to its ravages and the ways it is changing the face of medicine, making it difficult to say with certainty just what the effects of this pandemic will be for end-of-life care in the United States. While our current vantage point is limited by the cloud of uncertainty that inevitably surrounds a significant world event while one is still living through it, in the epilogue of this book we attempt to explore some of the lasting implications this pandemic may have for end-of-life care. What we can say for certain is that the way so many are dying in this country because of COVID-19—alone in the hospital without their loved ones by their side—only intensifies the plea we make in the pages that follow for health care professionals to honestly and courageously discuss how patients want the end of their lives to look, before they find themselves in a place where the choice is no longer theirs to make. This is especially true in a country and within a health care system that have historically avoided addressing the deeper existential questions surrounding suffering and death.

This book, then, intends to explore how and why US medicine has such a complicated relationship with death, seeming to embrace and deny its existence all at once. Palliative medicine is an official medical specialty, and hospice is a concept known to virtually all physicians. Yet nearly fifty years have come and gone since the hospice movement began, and there still remains a general confusion among both medical professionals and the US public about what hospice is (often seen as a "place people go to die" rather than a philosophy of care), its relation to palliative medicine, and who such care is intended for. And perhaps more concerning is how little the hospice movement has affected the way medicine is practiced, with physicians and nurses still participating regularly in "technologized" dying in intensive care units (ICUs) that focuses primarily on biological dysfunction—and with students, residents, and young clinicians woefully unprepared for the emotional reality of death and suffering, despite its presence at every turn.

For us, it's hard to delve into death and dying in the US medical system—a topic that is admittedly broad, complex, and for many, emotionally laden—without talking about our own experiences with our family, patients, students, residents, and colleagues, with the people whose identities and stories we have taken pains to anonymize (unless they have specifically requested otherwise), and whose willingness to be so open with us has been humbling and deeply rewarding. As a result, this book is both academic and personal: it's informed by research and intends to offer an accurate picture of the historical and social forces that shape the way we die, but it's also driven by personal experience, given the undeniable interconnectedness of our personal and professional lives.

Our hope is that what is written in the chapters that follow will offer readers a better understanding of what death and dying look like in the current world of US medicine as well as suggestions for what we can change within medical training and practice that will help all our caregivers authentically confront both the biological and existential realities of death in order to care well for their patients—and themselves.

DEATH AS MEDICAL FAILURE

It may seem a strange principle to enunciate as the very first requirement in a hospital that it should do the sick no harm.

—Florence Nightingale

Medical school did not prepare me for what it would be like to be a resident—a brand-new doctor making decisions for real patients. It took at least six months after graduation for me to stop looking over my shoulder to make sure people weren't talking to the person behind me when they started a sentence with "doctor."

When you're in medical school, the decisions you make for patients are never your own; there is always someone more senior than you checking your work and making sure you don't hurt anyone because of your naivete or hubris. Perhaps this was the reason I was so unprepared for failure when I began really taking care of patients during my residency—not my own failures necessarily, though I've had my fair share, and not even the failures of the medical system, though those failures are plenty. As strange as it sounds to say, especially for someone trained to care for sick people, I was completely unprepared for the inevitable failure of the human body.

While death was everywhere in medical school—cadavers and specimens and even dead patients—we never talked about human finitude or the fragility of being mortal. Instead, we learned about "fixing" biological breakdowns, how to detect physical or psychological pathology and effectively intervene. So I graduated from medical school as a full-grown adult with childlike notions of fixing and curing and saving—ideas shaped by heroic efforts I'd seen on TV shows. I thought that even when things went badly for patients, those of us in medicine would be there to turn things around and save the day. And I thought that in those rare cases when we couldn't save someone, we'd be angry and disappointed, we'd mumble a reluctant time of death, defeatedly stomp out of the room to find a distraught family, and offer the assurance that "we did everything we could."

This rescue fantasy did not seem improbable to me, in part because I'd seen patients seemingly come back from the dead before. I watched a cold, blue, seven-year-old boy pulled from his backyard pool leave the hospital four days later, laughing and waving as his parents paraded him down

As strange as it sounds to say, especially for someone trained to care for sick people, I was completely unprepared for the inevitable failure of the human body.

the hallway in a plastic red wagon. I saw a mother of three, whose lung infection would have undoubtedly killed her just years before the invention of the artificial lung that saved her life, leave the ICU and hug her young kids when they saw her for the first time in weeks. These were the things I'd expected to see in medical school, and I did see them—and they were more beautiful than I'd ever imagined.

But I was also there for the moments when we'd tried to rescue patients and couldn't, and these instances hurt worse than I'd ever imagined. In a way, I expected these moments too. I knew patients would die, despite our "heroism." What I wasn't prepared for—what no one ever told me I'd see—were the times when we would actively intensify pain and suffering, when we would break ribs during chest compressions and shove a breathing tube through vocal cords and down the larynx when there was no hope for recovery, when patients were old or fragile or terminally ill, or when they never wanted to die that way. After events like that, I didn't feel like I'd done something heroic at all. Mostly I felt guilty about what we had done—to those patients and their loved ones looking on.

Needless Violence

The reality of these situations became clearer to me during my early clinical experiences as a medical student in the emergency department (ED) of my university's hospital. Working in the ED was thrilling for a medical student. You'd see a wide variety of illnesses and problems, some of them dramatic and high energy. Even the less dramatic situations were exhilarating. I distinctly remember how during one of my first shifts, I had the chance to stitch a woman's hand that had been lacerated by a broken wine glass. Within minutes, I was in another room diagnosing mononucleosis as the underlying cause for a teenager's rash, which was due to an antibiotic someone prescribed for him thinking he had strep throat. I saw what I'd been studying in my textbooks come alive right in front of my eyes. And I loved it.

Later that same shift, we were notified that a patient would be coming in by ambulance because she was rapidly declining. As a young medical student, this news was both terrifying and exciting. In my mind, it seemed like an opportunity to learn how to handle a code blue, engage in resuscitative efforts, and save a life.

When our patient, Mrs. McGaugh, arrived, we learned that she was seventy-three years old and had end-stage kidney disease. She'd been dependent on renal dialysis for years to maintain kidney function and had decided to stop her dialysis treatments just six days before she came hurtling toward our emergency room in an ambulance. Someone at her house had called 911 when they saw that Mrs. McGaugh was confused and disoriented. Dialysis (or hemodialysis) requires a patient with end-stage kidney disease to be hooked up to a machine a few days a week since it serves as an artificial kidney, filtering wastes, eliminating excess fluids, and keeping things like electrolytes at normal levels in the blood. Hemodialysis, which had become widely available in the United States in the 1960s, is one of modern medicine's shining accomplishments, keeping patients alive despite their failed organs. But for those patients who elect to stop dialysis and have kidneys that are completely nonfunctional, they are likely to live only days to weeks. A recent study of nearly two thousand patients who discontinued dialysis found that they had an average life span of 7.4 days.[1]

At this point in my training, I had no idea why people would choose to stop something that was prolonging their life, and also had no idea what death would look like after stopping a life-sustaining therapy like hemodialysis. I'd only been taught how to prolong life, or at least improve mortality and stave off death for a while longer. And listening to lectures and studying books on how to do that, how to intervene and attempt to fix pathological biological breakdowns, was more than enough to keep me occupied all hours of the day and many hours of the night.

By the time Mrs. McGaugh showed up in our ED, I was already thinking how the team might best intervene to fix her body. Apparently she'd been growing confused and sleepy at home, so her daughter called the paramedics and asked that we do "everything we could" to help her mom.

When I saw Mrs. McGaugh being swiftly wheeled into one of the curtain-lined rooms in the ED, I was shocked when I glimpsed one of the skinniest people I'd ever seen. Her cheeks were quite literally hollow, and her eyes, which were only half opened and unseeing, sunk back into her skull. Her skin was ghostly pale and yellow, and her mouth was hanging open. She looked much more like the cadaver I'd dissected in the anatomy lab than any living person I'd ever seen. I had to squint my eyes to see the faintest rise and fall of her chest, and only seeing that with my own eyes could reassure me that she was, in fact, alive.

For just the briefest moment, I questioned whether a person who looked like Mrs. McGaugh could actually be resuscitated.

As they positioned the gurney into place, the paramedics gave a quick overview of Mrs. McGaugh's condition, repeating to the ED doctor what they'd said earlier about her daughter wanting us to "do everything we can to save her." Once the gurney's wheels were locked into place, two IVs were instantly placed in the veins of her arms, and the well-orchestrated concert of emergent resuscitation commenced. My job was to learn everyone else's job, know what to do, and know how to look for reversible causes of Mrs. McGaugh's unresponsiveness. That final task, however, was confusing to me. I wasn't quite sure Mrs. McGaugh's condition was reversible given that the underlying "reversible" cause of her looking so bad was her failing kidneys. And yet she had *elected* to stop her hemo-dialysis treatments. So then, wasn't her death expected? For what reason were we attempting to resuscitate her? To restart a heartbeat so that she could spend a few days on a breathing machine, largely unresponsive and incredibly uncomfortable until she eventually died from the kidney failure that was already happening?

Before I had a chance to coherently form these questions in my mind, the medical team jumped into action. They did what they'd been trained to do, and they did it well. Mrs. McGaugh's thin body cracked and heaved as a nurse, now standing on a step stool at the side of the bed, pressed her palms quickly and firmly into Mrs. McGaugh's chest two inches deep, just like I'd practiced on a mannequin a few months earlier. I watched as the resident at the head of the bed squeezed a bag attached to a mask that was over Mrs. McGaugh's mouth, forcing air into her lungs. Minutes later, it was obvious that the bag valve mask wasn't enough, and I tried to stay out of the way when I heard the attending physician in charge say that we needed to intubate the patient. I stared wide-eyed as the attending helped the resident with the intubation, tilting Mrs. McGaugh's head back and pushing a plastic tube into her mouth and down her throat. Silently, I stood aside for what felt like an eternity, watching her chest expand and collapse in heaving breaths.

I was startled back to reality by one of the nurse's booming voice, telling me that it was my turn to move over and start chest compressions. I nodded nervously in her direction before I shuffled over to the side of the bed, trying to stay out of the way of everyone else. A few seconds later, I placed my hands on Mrs. McGaugh's impossibly delicate chest bones. For the first few compressions, I recited the Bee Gees' "Staying Alive" in my head to ensure the right rhythm, around a hundred compressions per minute, just like I'd been taught. I concentrated intensely, trying to maintain circulation without completely crushing Mrs. McGaugh's frail chest.

I remember, however, looking up one time during my first turn at the side of the bed. From my new angle, I could see out the curtains and into the hall, where I saw who I assumed was Mrs. McGaugh's daughter with a young girl by her side. They seemed to stand there forever, looking on in horror, before a staff person guided them away toward a waiting room.

We worked away on Mrs. McGaugh's body, trading spots at the side of the bed, for nearly forty minutes before the time of death was finally called. When the attending called the time, no one stomped out of the room indignantly like I'd always imagined. No one seemed surprised that Mrs. McGaugh died despite our efforts. In fact, no one said anything at all. Every person left the room, except for one nurse who looked for a towel to cover Mrs. McGaugh's exposed body. I stayed back for a moment longer—just the nurse, our patient, and me in the tiny room together—in part because I didn't know what else to do.

As I finally turned to walk out, I glanced once more at the scene, Mrs. McGaugh's body in an unnatural pose, blood running down her arms from the IV sites, her lips, cracked and bleeding, pulled to one side by the intubation tube. With her head slightly turned toward me, Mrs. McGaugh seemed to gaze in my direction through half-opened lids with those same unseeing eyes I noticed nearly an hour ago.

I made my way out of the room and into the narrow hall, where I stood alone for a minute, bewildered by the whole thing. Why had we done all that to a woman who had almost no chance of meaningful recovery, who had chosen to stop the medical treatment that had been keeping her alive for years? Why did we inflict so much pain right before she died and potentially traumatize her daughter and granddaughter who looked on?

The simple answer is that we were asked to do it. The more unsettling answer is that for most of us in medicine, it's all we know to do.

Medicine's Rescue Fantasy

Doctors are trained to "cure" disease. Give them a disease, give them a physiological problem, and they, we, are equipped to try to fix it. While attempts are made in medical school to teach us about the psychosocial needs of patients, how to compassionately "break bad news," or how to listen to the patient's story, almost all medical students are taught within traditional accounts of medicine that see the body as an anatomical, biological, or biochemical structure that is best known and understood through the methods of science as well as the impartial observations of the medical professional.[2] Most students learn to intervene in order to restore a biological breakdown rather than to consider the complex dynamics of life that contribute to health and illness or to care well for patients whose bodies can no longer be treated or cured.

This might have been why I was so surprised to learn as a medical student that only about 15 to 20 percent of patients walk out of the hospital after a code like the one Mrs. McGaugh endured.[3] And that's a number for all patients of all ages, including healthy people who experience a trauma that requires resuscitation. This percentage decreases quickly with age and illness severity.[4] When it comes to a critically ill person with cancer in the ICU, the odds of walking out of the hospital after cardiopulmonary resuscitation (CPR) may be as low as 2.2 percent.[5] And for patients currently living in a nursing facility, the rate of survival beyond thirty days after a code is more like 2 percent.[6]

What is more, when someone's heart stops and they stop breathing, the process of "bringing back" the person does not often end well. Many patients will have broken ribs, with some studies suggesting that upward of 97 percent of patients end up with rib fractures.[7] And for those patients who do survive codes, poor quality of life after survival of CPR is common. In many cases, patients are left with a brain injury from cardiac arrest, with only 3 to 7 percent of patients able to return to their previous level of functioning after experiencing CPR in the hospital.[8]

Nevertheless, because CPR has and will continue to save some lives (just not nearly as many as most people think), it is now the standard of care in a hospital when someone is in cardiac or respiratory arrest. In other words, CPR is something that will happen to patients in the hospital who experience cardiac or respiratory arrest, unless the patient has specifically told them not to by declaring and formally documenting a code status of "do not resuscitate" (DNR).

Yet choosing one's status can be a bit complicated. A person can choose to be "full code," meaning take every measure to resuscitate them. Or they can choose DNR ("do not resuscitate"), or DNR/DNI ("do not resuscitate and do not intubate" or put on a ventilator). Or they can be a "limited code," where they decide what they would or would not like, a bit like an à la carte menu: CPR but no intubation, chest compressions but no IV medications, IV medications but no CPR, and so on.

If all that wasn't confusing enough, health care professionals often don't know a patient's code status (no one asked the patient), or they can't find where the code status is documented in the electronic health record (EHR).[9] In some hospitals, more than half the patients have an unknown code status or inconsistent documentation that makes it difficult to decipher what patients want should they stop breathing.[10] In cases like that, clinicians default to a full code—CPR, intubation, and IV drugs—even if the patient doesn't want it. To most health care professionals, the alternative (not resuscitating a person who *wanted* to be resuscitated) is simply unthinkable.

At the time that I encountered Mrs. McGaugh on my ED shift, I didn't yet know the dismal statistics associated with CPR. I also didn't know why someone would want to stop a treatment like kidney dialysis that could keep a person alive. So later on during my shift when I had some downtime, I decided to pull up Mrs. McGaugh's chart in the EHR to see if there was any indication of why she'd made the decision to stop dialysis. Because she'd been to both our hospital and university clinic before, I was able to access a lot of her medical history electronically. This was fortunate because had her outpatient clinic been outside our university system, accessing her records that night would have been impossible, as it would have required an official request for records and someone faxing physical records over. Because nearly all EHR systems are privately owned companies, and because they are all in competition with one another, they don't provide access to other EHR systems.[11] In some instances, a hospital and clinic in the same health system on the same medical campus that use two different EHRs are unable to share records electronically with one another—unless, of course, the hospital or clinic chooses to buy the same EHR as the other. Until then, however, they are limited to using things like fax machines and mailed paper records or CDs, making it nearly impossible to access test results or information from specialist visits in a timely manner.

While I was able to at least try to piece together Mrs. McGaugh's story because her records were in our system, doing so was not easy. Electronic records are notoriously difficult to navigate. Finding the specific information you're looking for can be tedious, given redundant clinician notes, lists of diagnoses and medications, and endless pages of lab results. So discovering anything about who Mrs. McGaugh was as a person before she died was like searching for the proverbial needle in a haystack. While most of the notes in her record contained a "social history" noting that Mrs. McGaugh was a nonsmoker who did not consume alcohol or drugs, it was hard to glean much else.

I was committed to my new self-assigned task, however. And with a lot more digging, I finally came across a note from a social worker that gave me some sense of Mrs. McGaugh's background. Apparently Mrs McGaugh was from New York City and moved to Arizona twenty years ago with her husband, Gerald. Together they'd had three daughters, two of whom lived locally, and eight grandchildren. Mrs. McGaugh used to work as a flight attendant and loved traveling and meeting new people, "but nothing compared to The City," the social worker quoted in the chart. She'd told the social worker that a lot had changed recently in the three years since Mr. McGaugh died from complications related to his diabetes. Since then, Mrs. McGaugh didn't get out much. Lately, the best part of her life was spending time with her grandchildren.

I was glad to get a better sense of who Mrs. McGaugh was, yet the other information in her record disturbed me. Embedded within the countless pages of data was a clear trend toward physical decline. In the last six months, Mrs. McGaugh had been hospitalized four times for infections, falls, and faints, and she also had steady weight loss, eventually becoming the seventy-nine-pound, five-foot, three-inch person who was brought to our ED. Along with this, I found a few quotes from Mrs. McGaugh documented by a hospitalist, the doctor who took care of her during her most recent hospital stay. It seems Mrs. McGaugh told the doctor that she didn't want any more dialysis treatments, explaining that she'd seen "how this goes with my Gerald." She'd said that she felt like too much of her time was spent getting treatments and that her body felt "too tired" to keep down that path. "Gerry suffered miserably in the hospital," she'd said. "I don't want to go out like that."

After piecing together Mrs. McGaugh's story, I remember feeling sort of stunned. It seemed obvious to me that Mrs. McGaugh was someone who understood what was happening to her and wanted to die outside the walls of the hospital. And the trends in her chart suggested that even without stopping her dialysis treatments, the end was not far off for her. Mrs. McGaugh was beginning to experience a profound loss of independence that prevented her from engaging in the parts of her life that mattered most. And after seeing what her husband went through, she did not want the end to look the same for her.

Nevertheless, no one ensured that the end would be different for Mrs. McGaugh. So she died the way she did in our ED. But why was this so? Why didn't her daughter know what she wanted? Had anyone talked to Mrs. McGaugh's family about what was going on with her? Had Mrs. McGaugh even talked to her family about it? Why didn't we, any of us in medicine who'd encountered her on her journey, support her in what seemed to be such a simple and reasonable request?

Making Wishes Known: It's Harder Than It Seems

Knowing patients' wishes—which can be outlined in documents called *advance directives*—helps us know what to do for patients in urgent situations, especially if patients

Why didn't we, any of us in medicine who'd encountered her on her journey, support her in what seemed to be such a simple and reasonable request?

are unable to make decisions for themselves. These documents are critical, particularly considering that doctors can find themselves in situations where they need to make decisions about end-of-life care for patients who are unable to articulate what they want. One large study in *The New England Journal of Medicine* found that over 70 percent of older adults who needed to make decisions about end-of-life care lacked decision-making capacity.[12]

In medicine, determining whether a patient has decision-making capacity is crucial since it dictates whether patients can make decisions for themselves or if someone needs to make decisions on their behalf. The four basic components of decisional capacity are a person's ability to *understand* the information presented, *appreciate* how this information applies to the situation, *reason* with this information, and *express a choice*.[13] It is not difficult to imagine the many ways patients can lose their decision-making capacity, including things like a sudden and severe stroke, the progressive loss of cognition from dementia, or even increased fatigue and confusion caused by a serious illness.

Advance directives are critical in this context since they are medical and legal documents that reflect patients' wishes should they become incapacitated and unable to articulate what kind of care they would want. There are essentially two major components of most advance directives: a document designating a surrogate medical decision maker (or medical power of attorney) who can represent the patient's wishes, and a document often referred to as a "living will" that lays out, in writing, patients' wishes for various medical situations, including whether they'd want to experience a full code, be on a ventilator, or have a feeding tube placed if they were unable to eat. The specifics of the documents vary among states and facilities, but the information they provide can give families or surrogate decision makers direction if they find themselves needing to make decisions on their loved one's behalf and can give clinicians direction if no one is present to speak for the patient.

After reviewing the note from the social worker and hospitalist in Mrs. McGaugh's record, it seemed she had clearly articulated her wishes to multiple practitioners. Nevertheless, like so many others, she did not write down her wishes. Despite the fact that Congress passed the Patient Self-Determination Act of 1990—requiring health care organizations to "inform patients of their rights under State law to make decisions concerning their medical care" as well as "periodically inquire as to whether a patient executed an advanced directive and document the patient's wishes regarding their medical care"—written advance directives are completed by a minority of patients.[14] A systematic review from 2017 showed that only about 37 percent of US adults have designated a medical power of attorney, and less than 30 percent have completed living wills.[15] And even among people with chronic illnesses, only 38 percent had completed advance directives.

While I'd like to believe that if patients like Mrs. McGaugh had only filled out advance directives, their wishes would've been known and respected, the reality is much more complicated. The reality is that much like a documented code status, it can be difficult for health care practitioners to access advance directives or find them in patients' records.[16] Sometimes the documents don't get scanned into the EHR, or sometimes they are scanned into the EHR at one hospital but not accessible in the EHR at another hospital. And in Arizona, where we live, a person can archive their advance directive documents in the secretary of state's Advance Directive Registry, but no one has access to those documents in the registry, other than the patient, who might be incapacitated when the documents are needed. So in emergent situations like Mrs. McGaugh's—even if patients *have* advance directives—the documents may be so difficult to find that patients still might receive unwanted, aggressive interventions at the end of life.

Though it seems like critical information about whether one would like to die in the hospital or not, or would like to be resuscitated or not, would be readily available to health care professionals, this is, too frequently, not the case. Too often, physicians are left making judgment calls in the midst of uncertainty, defaulting to "doing more," since the idea of not intervening when someone would've wanted more is a hard decision to live with. As a result, these default decisions are made even in circumstances where there is little to no chance of a patient's meaningful recovery, in part because these decisions align with much of our intervention-focused training, and in part because they feel like the safer bet when one considers facing a potential lawsuit for not "saving a life."

Add to this family dynamics, such as situations where loved ones want patients to continue to "fight" despite patients' desires to stop active treatment, and it can feel nearly impossible to honor a person's wishes at the end of life. While I cannot say for certain what transpired between Mrs. McGaugh and her daughter, it seemed to me that her daughter's request to "do everything" meant that she was either unaware of her mother's deliberate decision to stop dialysis, didn't understand *why* her mother would want to do so, or simply didn't understand what the process of dying would look like when her mother did stop dialysis. It was obvious there was no medical plan for how to support Mrs. McGaugh's hope to not "go out like that." Without clear communication and support between the health care team, the patient, and the patient's family, it makes sense that a daughter might call the paramedics in a panic and ask them to do everything they can to save her mother, despite what her mother really wanted.

Needless to say, there are real logistical reasons, system failures, and interpersonal dynamics that lead to someone like Mrs. McGaugh dying in a way she never would have wanted. But perhaps even more tragic than these material failures is the fact that the momentum created by medicine's preoccupation with fixes and cures and biological interventions is so relentless that even things like documented code statuses and accessible advance directives will never stop it.

Confronting Suffering

It was almost three years into medical school before I started to realize just how much the biological focus of medicine obscures the existential realities of illness, suffering, and death. From day one of my medical education, it was clearly—though implicitly—communicated that things like anatomy, biochemistry, physiology, and pharmacology are the real "stuff" of medicine and that one's efforts should be focused on grades, evaluations, and test scores. Being nice to patients and empathizing with their pain was not going to get any of us into competitive residency training programs; performing well on high-stakes tests, on the other hand, would.

On clinical rotations, when we really started seeing patients, most of us were preoccupied not with caring well for our patients but rather with looking good in front of our residents and attending physicians. "Looking good" meant being able to answer questions hurled your way by your superiors; it meant being efficient, memorizing and reciting information, formulating treatment plans, and teaching others information via informal and formal presentations. Spending extra time with patients not only failed to make us look good but also ran the risk of making us seem inefficient or aloof. There was no grade for authentically caring for others, and we knew it.

At the time, I remember thinking that this was simply part of the process—that I was making sacrifices now that would allow me to spend more time with patients later, after I graduated and had more control over my time. The trouble with this approach, however, is that the habits one forms during training inevitably shape one's future practice, regardless of good intentions. This is the insidious process by which empathy is slowly squeezed out of trainees and replaced by perceived needs for efficiency and detachment.[17] Trainees slowly lose sight of why they went to medical school in the first place; they get more comfortable interrupting patients during their stories and become increasingly focused on problems to solve rather than patients to care for.

I am confident I would have continued down this path of self-deception—thinking I would flip a switch and make more time for patients once I was a resident or practicing clinician—if I hadn't been forced to think otherwise. Fortunately for me, our school required us to take a course in ethics and medical humanities—a course that many of my classmates (including me at first) wrote off as unnecessary "fluff"—which began not long after my experience with Mrs. McGaugh and right around the same time I met Nicole. When I first met Nicole and asked what compelled her to move to Texas to pursue a PhD in medical humanities, she told me about her experience a few years earlier with her mom, who'd been diagnosed with terminal cancer. She told me what it was like for both of them to feel so confused and lost along the way, to feel caught off guard by her mom's death, despite the fact that it was always there, just around the corner. She told me how strange it was to be surprised by it, even when everyone knew it was inevitable, simply because no one was willing to talk about it.

It was conversations like these with Nicole and her friends in the graduate program, coupled with the emotional pangs that lingered after Mrs. McGaugh's death, that began to reveal to me medicine's confusing relationship with suffering and death. And this revelation made my new ethics and medical humanities course impossible to dismiss as extraneous. So I read the materials in earnest, engaged in discussions, and wanted to know more about the suffering of patients that exceeds the bounds of the biological body as well as the cultural, economic, political, and personal forces that make it so hard for mainstream medicine to confront this suffering.

While enrolled in our course in ethics and humanities, my classmates and I continued our other courses, one of which included seeing patients in the hospital with a team of residents and attendings. I was assigned to the oncology service, seeing patients with cancer who were sick enough to be hospitalized or whose chemotherapy treatments were so toxic they needed to stay in the hospital to be monitored and treated for severe side effects. During my second week with the team, we saw a new patient, a forty-one-year-old woman who'd come to the ED for pain caused by what turned out to be advanced breast cancer. The emergency medicine doctor she'd met the night before was the first doctor she'd seen about her illness, despite the fact that the cancer was so advanced, it had erupted through the skin of her breast and wrapped all the way around to the middle of her back. The disease inside her body was no less severe, having spread to her liver and lungs. When the oncologist on our team asked her why she had waited so long to seek care, she said she'd been too afraid—afraid to face the truth of her diagnosis and afraid that she wouldn't be able to afford treatment since she worked as a cashier at a small flower shop that didn't offer health insurance.

The time we spent with her that morning passed similarly to the time we spent with all the patients we saw during morning rounds; it was focused on treatments, next steps, plans, and side effects. The team was kind, but they were mostly informative and efficient. The team told her there was a chemotherapy she could try that might give her more time. The patient nodded her head with a shaky smile and undeniable fear in her eyes. She said her older sister was coming by later that morning, and she'd ask her if she could take care of her twelve-year-old son so she could start treatment.

When we left her room, I felt uneasy. I thought about Nicole and her mom, having conversations not unlike the one we just had, mere exchanges of information that fail to address real fears and concerns. Conversations about treatments that seem to inspire hope in the midst of despair, promising more time without qualifying just how much more. Conversations that fail to acknowledge the constant distress caused by the looming presence of death.

Now outside the patient's door, my team expressed their hesitations about treatment, doubting her ability to even tolerate the chemotherapy given how sick she was. I grew more uneasy with every word. I grew so uneasy, in fact, that I mustered the courage to voice my concerns out loud, telling the team I was worried our patient didn't fully understand that the treatment we just offered was not a cure and maybe she wouldn't want it if she knew how sick it would make her without actually curing her cancer.

My words hung embarrassingly in the air. Met with blank stares, I knew from that moment on to keep my concerns to myself. I regretted saying anything at all.

Later that afternoon, still unsettled by the situation, I decided I'd go back to the patient's room once we were finished with our work. I thought I might have a chance to talk to her and her sister. I wanted to talk to her about her worries; I wanted to give her a chance to talk about the fear that I so clearly saw in her face that morning. I had no idea what I was going to say, only that I was going to talk to them in the way I would want someone to talk to my own family.

When I walked in the patient's room, I stood near the doorway and introduced myself, telling her I was part of the big group who woke her up early that morning to talk. She said she remembered me and told me to come in. I sat in the chair near her bed and then told her that I thought it seemed like she had some questions about what we'd talked to her about earlier and maybe I could help answer some of them.

And that's all it took. Her doubts and hopes and worries spilled out. She told me how badly she wanted the treatment to work and how she feared it wouldn't. She told me she was worried for her son, who might not have a mother much longer. We talked about what it meant to have stage-four, incurable cancer. We talked about what she'd want to do if the treatment didn't work. And like so many patients I'd meet later on in my training, she told me she would want to know how limited her time was so that she could spend that time with her family.

She asked me a few questions, and I tried my best to answer the ones I knew. But mostly I just listened.

When I eventually got up to leave, she asked if she could give me a hug. I was glad she did because I wanted to ask her the same thing but didn't know if I should. As she held on to me a little longer, she thanked me for talking to her and then told me something I'll never forget: she said she was glad I came back to see her since I was the first person she'd met in the hospital who'd looked her in the eyes.

I wondered how that could be. I wondered why no one else was willing to acknowledge how scared she must've been. I wondered how a young, naive medical student who had nothing to offer in terms of skill or expertise could do anything to help her. And I wondered if she knew how much she taught me that day, helping me see that the conversations so many of us avoid—believing they're too difficult and time consuming, or that they'll upset patients or dash their hopes—are the exact conversations patients are longing to have.

I'd like to think it was moments like this one that eventually led me to a career in hospice and palliative medicine. And in a way, it was. Moments like that one—connecting with people and showing them care when they're most vulnerable—feel like the moments that motivate people to seek a career in medicine in the first place. Yet what I found during my training and even in my current practice is that these moments are rare. You'll miss them if

The conversations so many of us avoid are the exact conversations patients are longing to have.

you're not looking for them. And often you have to swim upstream, against the current of medical culture and practice, to find them.

Physician writers like Atul Gawande, Paul Kalanithi, and Jessica Nutik Zitter speak to what it's like to swim upstream.[18] They've written brilliant books that point to medicine's myopic focus on cure and highlight the need for a different kind of care. Gawande and Nutik Zitter, for instance, advocate for hospice care and palliative medicine, lauding their ability to offer whole person, compassionate care to patients, particularly those at the end of life. Their work has been critical in bringing to light medicine's strange relationship with aging and dying. And yet despite their work and the public attention it has brought to the way so many people die in the US medical system, what I have found in my own practice is that there is still much work to do. The principles guiding hospice and palliative medicine—whole person care, comfort, and quality of life—have not yet penetrated mainstream medicine. Every day, patients still die like Mrs. McGaugh, and doctors still have trouble looking patients in the eyes.

Just a few months ago, I took care of a seventeen-year-old kid who loved dry humor and playing the guitar, and who also was dying of brain cancer. Just two weeks before he died, he told me that what he feared the most was "the day all the doctors come in and no one can look me in the eye—and they tell me there's nothing more they can do."

This young kid knew what was in store for him; he knew there would come a time soon that his doctors would tell him there were no more options for him, that there was nothing else they could do to treat his brain tumor. Too frequently, it's at this crucial juncture that traditional disease-directed medicine leaves patients with the same resounding message: there is nothing more we can do. And so often, it is not until this final moment, bereft of hope, that someone like me in palliative medicine is called in at the eleventh hour to walk alongside patients on their final journey when we've only just met.

DEATH AND DYING IN WESTERN CULTURE

Suffering is only intolerable when nobody cares.

—Dame Cicely Saunders, founder of the modern hospice movement

A few years before I met Shawn and heard his countless stories of patients and families who meet a palliative medicine doctor—a stranger—when "there's nothing more to do," I lived through the experience myself.

I was a young college student when my mom was diagnosed with advanced ovarian cancer. While I grew up with my mom being a nurse, I knew surprisingly little about medicine or hospitals. Becoming my mother's primary caregiver, however, I quickly learned how to manage nausea, assist with showers, style wigs, control pain after high-risk surgeries, drain chest tubes, and dress deep wounds. I learned which detergent was best for blood or vomit, which colostomy bags adhered best, and how to sneak extra calories into meals that were left mostly untouched. The one thing I never learned, though, was how to face the fact that the woman I most adored on this earth was dying.

Perhaps I had assumed that when it was time to face the unfathomable, someone other than the two of us would bring it up. Perhaps I thought that the doctors who treated her cancer for over two years would know her well enough to recognize when things weren't looking good. But perhaps they knew us well enough to know how terrified we were and see how badly I didn't want to talk about how I was losing my mother forever. Perhaps they noticed how I was trying to "protect" her, how I made a point to attend every single one of her appointments because I knew she wouldn't bring up the idea of dying while I was in the room. Perhaps they were simply following our lead, regardless of the fact that we were headed down a path paved with fear, exhaustion, and unchecked hope.

And so my mother's oncologists never talked to her about the fact that she was dying. In fact, during her final hospital stay, just sixteen hours before she died, one oncologist offered her a fourth-line chemotherapy that he said might work. Two hours later, another oncologist came in to ask her if she'd like to change her code status to DNR. I sat on my makeshift bed on the hospital room floor confused when I heard my mother say yes. I didn't understand why she would want to give up when there might be another treatment left. I was haunted by visions of her dying without me during the few times I left her side to go home to shower and pack more clothes. I thought that CPR could bring her back to me, alive and alert, and then she could die later when I was there with her.

I asked her if she might want to reconsider the DNR decision given that there could be a chance she'd stop breathing and need CPR when I wasn't with her. She said she was sure she wanted to keep the DNR. She was a nurse after all; she knew too much.

Later that same afternoon, a palliative medicine doctor we'd never seen before came in to talk to us. He told my mom that he saw her scans and things "didn't look good." He said he wanted her to be comfortable and more chemotherapy would likely make her feel worse without shrinking the cancer at all. I sat by, stunned and angry. I hated him for talking about this with her. I thought his ideas about "being comfortable" were premature. He didn't know my mom and didn't know what she wanted. I felt like every word out of his mouth was hopeless and hurtful and unhelpful.

I was certain my mom felt the same way. So one could imagine my surprise when after only fifteen minutes with this doctor, my mom made the decision to move to an inpatient hospice facility in the morning for a few days before transitioning home so that she could spend her last weeks there with us. I couldn't believe that the decision was made so quickly and wasn't sure she was ready to move in that direction.

The instant the doctor left the room, however, my mom started to cry and said how relieved she was to not have to "fight" anymore. Everything was happening so fast. Instinctually, I crawled into the bed with her, telling her how glad I was that she felt that way, that I hated that I was losing her, but that I was grateful she felt so much peace about it. I said it would be good to get back home and be together as a family for whatever time she had left.

My mom never got to see our home again. In fact, she never left the hospital. In the early hours of the following morning, the sun rose over the desert mountains and flooded her hospital room, which was also flooded by twenty or more of our friends and family. They surrounded her and sang to her, kissed her forehead, and told her how much she meant to them. A friend was there to explain to me what was happening to my mom's body and how things would look and change as death got closer. She only knew what to tell me because she had recently watched her dad die.

As the hours passed, I worried that there were too many of us in the room and hallway, that we were in the way, that we were being too loud. *There aren't supposed to be this many visitors in a hospital room*, I thought to myself, wondering if someone would come in and ask us to keep it down. But no one did. We didn't see much in the way of others that morning. We never saw my mom's doctors again, with the exception of the palliative medicine doctor who quietly stepped into the room that morning to see if there was anything he could do for us before gently patting my mother's legs as if to say goodbye to the woman he'd just met.

And then, finally, just after nine in the morning, I again lay in my mom's hospital bed, my head on her chest, listening to the final beats of her heart, trying to sear in my mind the way her skin felt, the way her hands looked, the softness of her short, fuzzy hair. I told her I hoped to be more like her, to love people the way she did. I told her that it was OK, that she could go. And then she was gone from this world forever, just like that.

Looking back at that time, I have a strange sense of shame that my mom died in the hospital instead of at home. I remember I had the same feeling then in the hospital room too—as if we were doing something "wrong," as if it would have been uncomfortable for the other patients and their families on the oncology floor to have known that someone was dying so near to them in the same space in which they were supposed to recover and walk out better than they walked in. The hospital is a place to be fixed and rescued, a place where people only die in the ED after heroic efforts—not a place where families cram into small rooms, navigating IV poles and tubes and machines to bear witness to their loved one's last moments on earth.

In the hospital, death is everything and it's nothing. Death—that is, preventing its occurrence—is the ultimate benchmark by which the hospital measures its work. Extraordinary efforts are made to prevent death, control it, and slow down its appearance. And yet when death does make its appearance, the silence around it can be deafening. When someone dies in the hospital, there is no pomp, no ceremony, no vigil. There is merely more work to do and more patients to see.

But how did we get here? How did hospitals and nursing facilities become the places where more than half of the people in the United States die, despite their impersonal nature and the fact that the majority of the US population (65 to 70 percent) say they would prefer to die at home?[1] And how did this happen so quickly? Less than a century ago, most deaths occurred at home, and the hospital played little to no part in care for the dying. What changed in the last sixty years that led to my mom dying in the hospital instead of at home and transformed dying from a natural, familial event into a medicalized, institutionalized process?

The Rise of the Modern Hospital and the Institutionalization of Death

"Suddenly, it seemed in the late 1960s," notes historian Charles Rosenberg, "the American hospital became a

When someone dies in the hospital, there is no pomp, no ceremony, no vigil. There is merely more work to do and more patients to see.

problem." Inside the walls of the new modern hospital, technology, bureaucracy, and professionalism coexisted alongside things like birth, death, suffering, and pain, resulting in an "institution clothed with an almost mystical power, yet suffused with a relentless impersonality." Rosenberg's description of the modern hospital is a far cry from the hospital of the previous centuries—an "insignificant aspect of American medical care" where physicians could offer little in the way of surgery or therapeutic intervention.[2] In fact, most of the sick during those earlier times were cared for by the family, with the exception of the severely ill or poor, who would most likely find themselves in almshouses, not hospitals.[3] Almshouses, which were founded in the United States as early as the seventeenth century, were unspecialized welfare institutions that provided care for the elderly, poor, orphaned, and (only incidentally) sick.[4]

Throughout the eighteenth and early nineteenth centuries, there were few general hospitals that exclusively cared for people who were sick. According to French historian Philippe Ariès, it was also during this time that death in the Western world, which almost exclusively occurred at home, was experienced socially and relationally with others in the community. Death was a public event and one that represented the transition out of the suffering of the fleshly world into the beauty of the (Christian) afterlife. While this transition into the pain-free and sinless afterlife was something to be desired, mourning among the bereaved was expected and encouraged. The period of mourning that followed a death was filled with visits from family, friends, and community members, for it "was not only an individual who was disappearing but society itself who had been wounded and that had to be healed."[5]

As the nineteenth century progressed, however, descriptions of the "beautiful" death began to shift, as notions of death as ugly, frightening, or dirty began to take hold, and a new emphasis on hygiene, sterility, and cleanliness affected care for the dying.[6] After the Civil War, for instance, reformers concerned with the squalid condition of the almshouses made efforts to differentiate these institutions by sending the sick and dying to separate facilities to receive care. In some cities, public hospitals evolved out of these new almshouse infirmaries, while separate charity hospitals (funded by voluntary contributions) developed alongside them. The continued existence of the old almshouses served an important function for these newly established public and charity hospitals. Those who had contagious, chronic, or incurable illnesses, or those merely deemed unworthy or undeserving of care, were sent away to the old almshouses in an attempt to "give these new hospitals a more attractive identity and to make them safer and more acceptable." The exclusion of these patients served to keep down mortality rates, and more important, defy the traditional image of the hospital as a "house of death."[7]

Throughout most of the nineteenth century, care in these new hospitals offered no real advantages over care in the home, and physicians were hesitant to admit patients because of the frequent spread of infection on the wards. Yet increased concern about ventilation and cleanliness allowed hospitals to emerge from disrepute even before any major technological advances materialized. This new focus on cleanliness was in large part a result of the work of Florence Nightingale, English social reformer and founder of modern nursing. By concentrating her efforts on hygiene and ventilation, Nightingale was able to dramatically reduce the death rate from infection of British soldiers in military hospitals during the Crimean War in the 1850s.[8] Soon after the war, Nightingale and other reformers brought these same strategies to the hospital in an attempt to reduce the high levels of hospital infection. For Nightingale, the hospital—though unlikely to offer *cure*—should at least offer a clean environment that would prevent the spread of infection and promote natural healing.[9]

It would not be long, however, before the promise of cure would become a defining characteristic of the hospital. Germ theory, confirmed by Robert Koch in 1876, suggested that specific germs invaded the body and multiplied, ultimately causing disease. And although scientific knowledge had already played a central role in the delivery of medical care at this time, the emergence of germ theory not only reshaped the hospital but also transformed every aspect of medicine.[10] Sterile procedure and aseptic surgery, for instance, led to a dramatic improvement in surgical outcomes, and the practice of surgery became increasingly more prestigious as it offered more and more promises of the restoration of health. In fact, by the turn of the twentieth century, surgical admissions to the hospital began to outnumber medical admissions as people in the United States started to more readily and perhaps eagerly "accept the hospital."[11] The success of aseptic surgery alongside the ability to offer new "cures," as well as the development of the on-site hospital laboratory and new technology like the X-ray machine, transformed hospitals from "places of dreaded impurity and exiled human wreckage into awesome citadels of science and bureaucratic order."[12]

As a result of these changes, families increasingly came to depend on the hospital, and the strangers within it, at times of illness and impending death.[13] Both the new image of the hospital and changing ideas about disease informed by germ theory seemed to offer a sense of certainty for patients wading through the insecurity and fear that so often come with pain and illness. As Rosenberg suggests,

> Prospective patients were influenced not only by the hope of healing, but by the image of a new kind of

medicine—precise, scientific, and effective. For the first time, patients came to their physician with the hope—and increasingly the assumption—that he might *impose* and not merely facilitate healing.[14]

Historically, scholars have attributed the shift from the home to the hospital as the site of death to the introduction of increasingly specialized medical technology.[15] Although new technology along with new surgical and therapeutic interventions offer a partial explanation for the rise of the hospital as well as the institutionalization of death and dying, medical historians suggest that the *idea* of scientific progress is just as important, if not more so, than the technology itself.[16] Medicine's ability to offer the "hope of secular healing" in a modern world that had grown increasingly rationalist, individualized, and irreligious helped legitimize the role of the physician and ever-expanding position of the hospital in society.[17] The hospital's rise to power and its becoming the "appropriate" site for death were not the result of technological advancement alone but rather the combination of technological developments, a cultural desire for scientific certainty and progress, and the vested interests of those who desired to professionalize the practice of medicine. And so by the first few decades of the twentieth century, both the hospital and the physicians within it had replaced the home and family as the site for managing health, illness, and death.[18]

Hidden Death in the Hospital

After the care of the sick—and therefore the care of the dying—became largely institutionalized in the early years of the 1900s, the allure of scientific progress continued well into the twentieth century. As US life superficially returned to "normal" after the Second World War, and ideas of mass casualties and destruction began to fade, there lingered a sense that maybe death, too, could be left on the battlefield.[19] And when Howard Florey and his Oxford colleagues purified Alexander Fleming's penicillin compound in 1941, it would be hailed as "the most glamorous drug ever invented."[20] As the US public read about the discovery of such "wonder drugs" and other "miracles" of modern medicine, they were confronted with evidence suggesting that life was indeed getting better.[21] Advances in medicine seemed to be an unstoppable force, and physicians gained even greater respect and admiration during the first half of the twentieth century, which came to be known as Western medicine's "golden age."[22]

Although complaints about the coldness and impersonality of the hospital were already being voiced by the first decades of the twentieth century as the use of medical technology became more common, they were intensified during the golden age as science and technology took center stage while many patients were reduced to the pathology behind their symptoms.[23] What is more, new technological advances led to unanticipated dilemmas for both physicians and ethicists. With the introduction of the positive pressure ventilator in the 1950s, for instance, patients who might have otherwise died from a devastating illness or injury could now maintain heart and lung function with mechanical ventilation. While this advancement was hugely beneficial for patients with reversible conditions, it also meant that patients who had no chance of a meaningful recovery could be kept alive via ventilation, medications, and tube feedings, sometimes for years after their illness or injury.

With this new technology, the line between life and death was blurred. Historically, death was determined by the cessation of heart and respiratory function. But by the 1960s, medical professionals started talking about "brain death," a term that is still confused today with things like a coma or disorders of consciousness (such as a persistent vegetative state or unresponsive wakefulness syndrome).[24] Unlike a coma or disorder of consciousness where patients can breathe on their own, patients with brain death do not have a functioning brain stem and cannot breathe—and therefore cannot live—without a ventilator. And unlike patients in a coma who might recover fully, patients with brain death have no brain activity, and this lack of activity is permanent; they will not wake up or regain any awareness. So even while new medical advances could keep a patient's heart beating and lungs breathing, that patient might be considered dead by accepted medical standards.[25]

Given the shifting definitions and clinical criteria for death, it may not be surprising that David Sudnow, a sociologist who studied hospital deaths in the 1960s, found that within the walls of the hospital, death was primarily conceived of in scientific and biological terms.[26] The hospital death was stripped of all metaphysical and existential meaning and viewed instead as a "technical failure . . . an inability of modern medicine to effect a cure."[27] As medical ethicists Thomas Cole and Nathan Carlin note, the practice of scientific medicine at this time had detached itself from broader frameworks of meaning and value and "was not intellectually equipped to handle the moral and existential questions produced by its power."[28]

In his 1967 work *Passing On: The Social Organization of Dying*, Sudnow reported his findings of what he calls the first ethnographic study of "death work"—that is, the daily working life of hospital staff who care for the dying— and describes the distance and detachment on the wards of two US hospitals. Sudnow explains that patient deaths were discussed freely and openly among hospital staff, though these deaths were often spoken of with a sense of routinized indifference. He recounts the following conversation between two floor nurses:

A: I hope it's a quiet night. I'm not too enthusiastic.

B: They all died during the day today, lucky us, so you'll probably have it nice and easy. . . . Can you believe it, we had five deaths in the last twelve hours.

A: How lovely.

B: Well, see you tomorrow night. Have fun.[29]

Sudnow goes on to describe how many dying patients in the 1960s experienced "social death" in the hospital long before their physical death, as hospital staff no longer saw terminal patients as possessing "socially relevant" attributes and "regarded [them] as already a corpse."[30] He recounts instances of physicians filling out autopsy permits prior to patients' deaths and a moment when he witnessed a nurse repeatedly and "somewhat forcefully pushing [a dying patient's] eyelids together" while the patient was still alive because, as the nurse explained, it was simply "more difficult to accomplish a complete lid closure" after death in order to make sure the body "resemble[d] a sleeping position."[31]

Sudnow depicts how physicians often kept their distance from dying patients and how it was not uncommon for hospital staff to attempt to deny or disguise death's occurrence on the wards, especially in the presence of other patients. There were many times when a dying patient was quickly moved to a private room, where after death, a nurse would "post on the door a blank slip of white paper, which is understood by hospital staff that a dead body lies inside." And in cases where a patient died unexpectedly and was not successfully hidden before death, hospital staff went to great lengths to conceal the death from onlookers:

> When the dead patient is removed from the room, some care must be taken to cover the possibility that others might see the patient as he is removed, and often an attempt is made to make him look alive. On repeated instances, variations on the following example were observed: a nurse came into the room with an aide and pretended to be talking to the patient. "Let's go to X-ray," she said, whereupon, with the assistance of the aide, the patient was transferred from the bed to the stretcher. . . . Usually, such removal can go unnoticed. . . . On occasion, however, a live patient makes some skeptical comment about the dead one, who is being passed off as live, like "Didn't he just go to X-ray?" at which point personnel attempt to give an answer that will allow them to meet the requirement of getting the body out without directly confronting the live patient with the fact that it is a [dead] body.[32]

Just as often as death was rendered invisible for onlookers, terminal diagnoses were concealed from dying patients themselves.[33] This phenomenon, which was common in US medicine during the mid-twentieth century, is also described in Barney Glaser and Anslem Strauss's well-known work *Awareness of Dying*, which they published in 1965 after researching for three years how dying patients were treated in the hospital. Writing during a time when "senseless prolonging of life within hospital walls by medical technology [ran] wild," Glaser and Strauss drew the public's attention to the problems that arise when health care professionals, and the US culture at large, assume that "life is preferable to whatever may follow it," and thus avoid discussing death and dying. According to Glaser and Strauss, the most common way of addressing death and dying in the hospital involved both physician and patient engaging in a "mutual pretense" wherein "both agree[d] to act as if he were going to live." Like Sudnow, Glaser and Strauss suggest that one of the reasons behind this approach to dying was medicine's preoccupation with the scientific and technical aspects of care that overshadowed the human elements of sickness and suffering. As they put it,

> In hospitals, as in medical and nursing schools,
> discussion of the proper ways to manage dying
> patients tends to be only in strictly technical medical

and nursing terms. . . . Physicians and nurses understandably develop both standardized and idiosyncratic modes of coping with the worst hazards. The most standard mode . . . is a tendency to avoid contact with those patients.[34]

In part because medicine was ill equipped to handle existential questions, and in part because of the technical and curative focus of mainstream medical care, dying patients were often intentionally left in ignorance about their terminal diagnoses.[35] As a result, many patients received unwanted and invasive treatment at the end of life, leading to a painful and prolonged death.[36] In remaining silent and offering dying patients unrealistic hope of eventual healing, physicians simultaneously had everything and nothing to do with death and dying. Although medicine had taken death within its scope and accepted death's biological reality, it seemed to avoid its emotional and existential realities. The modern hospital—similar to the early hospital of the nineteenth century that confined the dying to almshouses in an attempt to reinvent itself—was not intended for dying patients, despite the fact that it brought them there in the first place. In many ways, then, hospitalized patients were not so much in denial of death as they were denied a space in which to openly die.

Patients were not
so much in denial of
death as they were
denied a space in
which to openly die.

THE DEATH AND DYING MOVEMENT

If there is a meaning in life at all, then there must be a meaning in suffering. Suffering is an ineradicable part of life, even as fate and death. Without suffering and death, human life cannot be complete.

—Viktor E. Frankl

In Ariès's perspective, death and dying became such a problem for Western culture in the twentieth century because as medicine and science progressed, death was among the few things on earth that humankind could not control. The response, then, was to either deny its existence—render it invisible within the hospital, and slowly eliminate elaborate funeral processions and public displays of mourning, for instance—or accept death as a technical fact, a biological failure and nothing more.[1] And with nearly 53 percent of people dying in the hospital by

1964, these two responses to death became commonplace in medicine.[2]

Yet it wasn't long before public exposés, like those of Sudnow as well as Glaser and Strauss, brought the public's attention to the crisis of institutionalized dying. These exposés were likely incited by the death and dying movement, which had appeared on the US landscape in the late 1950s in response to the idea that death had become "taboo" in the West and the United States in particular.[3] English anthropologist Geoffrey Gorer, for example, garnered international attention with his 1955 essay "The Pornography of Death," which claimed that death had become just as shameful and unmentionable as sex had been during the Victorian era.[4] Death as a normal life process had been made invisible and was replaced with objectionably obscene or violent representations in film and television. Gorer argued that while contemporary Western society may have become accustomed to seeing violent deaths in the media, few talked about or saw firsthand the death of a loved one in real life. This may have been why people in the United States found the exposés by Sudnow and others— which depicted the real experiences of dying patients in the hospital—so compelling.

It would be misguided, though, to assume that it wasn't until the mid-twentieth century that death became taboo in the West. Ariès notes that things actually began to shift, albeit more subtly, in the eighteenth and early nineteenth centuries when the pain and unruliness of death was circumvented by "beautifying" it. Death and the dying person were exalted during this time, as death was seen as bringing both the triumphal end of suffering and a passage to the refuge of eternal life. The bereaved mourned together, finding solace in ideas about fraternal reunions and the beauty of the afterlife. Beautifying death, however, became more difficult by the mid-twentieth century not only because public and communal engagement with the dying had almost disappeared but also because it was difficult to find beauty in the experience of dying "in a tangle of tubes all over [the] body, breathing artificially," as Ariès puts it.[5]

While it's difficult for some to pinpoint exactly why the United States became transfixed with death and death denial in the mid-twentieth century, for Ariès the explanation is rather simple: the medicalized, technologized dying of the modern era was too monstrous to ignore. As he observed in 1977, "Shown the door by society, death is coming back in through the window."[6]

The Birth of Modern Hospice Care

Things have undoubtedly changed since the time these sociologists and historians were describing hospitalized deaths to the time when my own mother died in the hospital. Despite the fact that the immanence of my mom's death was a surprise to us, no one overtly lied to her about her condition. No one filled out an autopsy report or tried to force her eyes closed before she died. No one tried to hide her away in a secluded hospital room to die alone. Unlike patients in the past, hospice was an option for us, and had we pursued it, she could have had a death that was more aligned with the way she had lived. What is concerning, however, is that a real conversation about what transitioning to hospice would mean or actually look like never occurred. And we certainly didn't know about palliative medicine—a medical specialty dedicated to treating symptoms, managing pain, and offering psychosocial support, even while patients are still receiving active treatment. We didn't know about this option and that my mom could have received this kind of care at the beginning of it all, right after her diagnosis. As a result, my mom often had uncontrolled nausea and vomiting, weakness, fatigue, lack of appetite, and intense pain that we simply accepted as part of the disease process. What's worse is that no one talked to my mom or our family about her goals of care or how she hoped to live during the limited time she had left. In fact, we were never really told just how limited that time was.

Nevertheless, the way my mom died was much more humane than I imagine it would have been fifty years ago. This is in large part the result of the death and dying movement in the United States, and more specifically, the critically influential hospice movement that later arose from it. Elisabeth Kübler-Ross, a Swiss American psychiatrist whose seminal work *On Death and Dying* (1969) laid the groundwork for many of the grassroots organizations in support of providing quality, patient-centered care at the end of life, is closely associated with the death and dying movement. Her status as a physician and gift for public speaking allowed her to quickly become one of the major figureheads of the movement in the United States.[7] After completing the research for her book, which included interviewing countless dying patients and developing her legendary "five stages" of death, Kübler-Ross called for medicine to "refocus on the patient as a human being." Claiming that medicine had "changed greatly in the last decades," Kübler-Ross asks,

> Is our concentration on equipment, on blood pressure, our desperate attempt to deny the impending death which is so frightening and discomforting to us that we displace all our knowledge onto machines, since they are less close to us than the suffering face of another human being, which would remind us once more of our lack of omnipotence, our own limits and failures, and last but not least perhaps our own mortality? . . . Are we becoming more human or less human?[8]

Largely inspired by Kübler-Ross's work, advocates for improving end-of-life care started to make headway in public discourse. Though there were no hospice programs anywhere in the United States as the country entered the 1970s, this would soon change as people committed to transforming care for the dying began to look to the United Kingdom for direction.[9] The first modern hospice facility in the United Kingdom—St. Christopher's Hospice in southwest London—was established in 1967 by the founder of the modern hospice movement, Dame Cicely Saunders. Born in 1918 in North London, Saunders originally enrolled at Oxford to study politics, philosophy, and economics shortly before the Second World War.[10] At the start of the war, however, Saunders left Oxford to enroll as a student at Nightingale School of Nursing. She practiced nursing for several years until issues with her back, which she had struggled with for years, forced her to leave the field. She returned to Oxford, where she studied to become a medical social worker.

While working at Archway Hospital as a social worker, Saunders met David Tasma, a forty-year-old refugee from Poland who was dying of cancer. Saunders and Tasma grew close in the final weeks of his life, and the time she spent with him addressing his physical, emotional, social, and spiritual pain—what she would later refer to as "total pain"—instilled in her a vision for better care for the dying.[11] After his death, Tasma left Saunders five hundred pounds, a significant amount at that time, to help her realize her vision of creating a home that would provide care for the dying.

After this experience, Saunders began volunteering as a nurse at St. Luke's Hospital in North London in an effort to learn more about the specific needs of patients at the end of life. She took the night shift since it required less lifting of patients and allowed her to work despite her back pain. While there, she became increasingly distressed by what she perceived as doctors' neglect of patients with terminal illnesses.[12] Saunders spoke of this with a surgeon colleague who agreed with her assessment—though it was his belief that the best way for Saunders to address this issue was to become a physician herself. So in 1951, at the age of thirty-three, Saunders enrolled in medical school. She completed her medical degree in 1957 and became the first modern doctor to devote her career to dying patients.[13]

By the time St. Christopher's Hospice was created in 1967, Saunders had been writing about end-of-life care for nearly a decade. One of her most well-known works, "Dying of Cancer," was published in 1958 when Saunders was still a medical student. In this article, Saunders called on physicians to not abandon dying patients and "remain the center of the team who work together to relieve where they cannot heal."[14] This piece became a manifesto of sorts for the subsequent hospice care movement as it laid out some of the major issues related to caring for the dying that now seem so familiar: general pain management, addressing mental and emotional distress along with spiritual needs, and informing patients and relatives about diagnoses and prognoses.

When the first hospice opened in the United States in 1974 in New Haven, Connecticut, complete with a home care program and forty-four bed inpatient facility, the United States finally had its own shining example of the new hospice vision.[15] Staying true to the values of Saunders, new US hospices made it clear that hospice was not a facility but instead an approach to care. Like palliative medicine, hospice provided and still provides comfort care for patients and support for families. But unlike palliative care, patients must have a terminal illness and be likely to die within six months in order to enroll in hospice, and any attempts to cure a person's illness are almost always stopped once the person is enrolled.

Because hospice is a *philosophy* of care, it is not tied to a specific place and can be offered at home or in a facility like a nursing home, hospital, or separate inpatient hospice center.[16] While in places like Canada, "hospice" more specifically refers to an actual place—that is, a physical building where patients can receive care at the end of life—in the United States, hospice organizations emphasize providing care in patients' homes. Hospice nurses make home visits regularly in an effort to get to know patients personally in order to help them live out the rest of their time in the ways they wish. These nurses also offer help and guidance to patients' primary caregivers, usually a family member or friend, who manage their loved ones' care and provide the hands-on, around-the-clock care. With the help of their caregivers and hospice nurses, patients usually live out the rest of their lives at home and are only admitted to inpatient hospice facilities for short periods of time if their pain or other symptoms are too complex to manage at home, or to offer respite care for their caregivers.[17]

In an effort to address "total pain" and care for patients as whole people, hospice care brings together a team of people—like nurses, doctors, social workers, chaplains, and trained volunteers—to work with patients and their families or caregivers to provide medical, emotional, and spiritual support. When they were first introduced, these standards for end-of-life care quickly spread throughout the nation and were so well received that they eventually became part of the US government's Medicare Hospice Benefit that was established in 1982 through amendments to the Social Security Act, offering reimbursement for participating hospice programs. By 1984, only a decade after the establishment of the first US hospice facility, over a thousand hospice organizations had opened across the country.[18]

Hospice care brings together a team to work with patients and their families to provide medical, emotional, and spiritual support.

Contemporary Issues in End-of-Life Care

Undoubtedly, hospice care and its focus on limiting aggressive and futile treatment at the end of life have made great strides in changing how hospitalized patients die as well as in helping more people die at home. In fact, for the first time in the twentieth century, more people are dying at home than in the hospital.[19] According to the Centers for Disease Control, in 2016, over 30 percent of those who died in the United States did so at home, and around 8 percent died in an inpatient hospice care facility rather than in the hospital.[20] And with the establishment of palliative medicine as a formal medical specialty in 2006, more patients are experiencing the benefits of palliative care—like having their pain and symptoms expertly addressed, having their goals articulated, and even *living longer* with a terminal illness than they would without palliative care.[21] Studies have shown that the interdisciplinary approach to care that hospice and palliative medicine offer, with their teams of doctors, nurses, social workers, chaplains, pharmacists, nursing aides, and other professionals, allows them to provide whole-person care, ultimately improving not only physical but also psychosocial symptoms, along with increasing patient satisfaction and caregiver well-being, even during bereavement.[22] What is more, adequately addressing patients' pain and symptoms in the outpatient setting can prevent or reduce hospital stays, and meeting with patients and families in the hospital can promote clearer goals of care, more tailored treatments, and more comprehensive discharge plans for transitioning home from the hospital. As a result, hospice and palliative medicine can actually reduce expensive and avoidable hospitalizations, readmissions, and emergency department visits at the end of life.[23] Put simply, hospice and palliative medicine can and do provide better, more comprehensive care for patients and their families, and they do so in a way that saves patients, families, and health care systems money.

Despite the fact that patients can live longer and have improved quality of life when they receive hospice or palliative care, some people still equate hospice with "giving up" or "the place people go to die." Indeed, some people even associate hospice care with physician-assisted suicide, or what the American Public Health Association calls "aid in dying."[24] It's important to distinguish aid in dying from the work of hospice, especially because the development of aid in dying in the early 1990s may have been a response to inadequate end-of-life care, as a plea of sorts for better and *more* care at the end of life, not less. While aid in dying has been legally practiced in the United States for over two decades—starting in Oregon in 1997—and it is now legal in nine US states and the District of Columbia, aid in dying is not typically associated with the work of hospice care, despite the fact that aid in dying is—like hospice—only available to patients with terminal illnesses who are likely to die within six months, at least in the United States.[25]

Patients who are residents of states where it is legal and request aid in dying must receive an in-depth evaluation from a physician, who must ensure that patients have full decisional capacity as well as explore the physical, psychological, spiritual, financial, and social issues influencing a patient's request.[26] Once all this is completed, and it is determined that a patient is fully aware of other end-of-life care options and still chooses aid in dying, a physician who is willing may write a patient a prescription for life-ending medication that can be taken when and where the patient decides, and often without a physician present.

While the American Medical Association's Council on Ethical and Judicial Affairs voted in 2019 to leave in place the association's current policy that physicians should not participate in what it notably calls "physician-assisted suicide" because it is "fundamentally incompatible with the physician's role as healer," the American Academy of Hospice and Palliative Medicine has taken a "position of studied neutrality" on the issue.[27] In its statement, the academy makes a point to distinguish aid in dying from hospice and palliative care, highlighting that palliative care "relieves suffering without intentionally hastening death," but it also acknowledges that physicians practicing in jurisdictions where it is legal may help patients die—though they should never feel obligated to do so and should "ensure their actions are consistent with best available practices that limit avoidable suffering through end of life."[28]

Recently, some hospice organizations in places like California and Washington State have made the decision to allow their hospice physicians to both consult on a request for aid in dying and be with patients before and after they ingest a lethal prescription.[29] While none of these hospices want to be perceived as destination locations for aid in dying, some do want to ensure that patients who choose aid in dying while enrolled in hospice do not feel that they are abandoned by their care team after making the decision to end their life. Yelena Zatulovsky, for instance, the vice president of patient experience at a hospice organization with locations in states including California, Oregon, and Colorado, explained in a recent *Medscape* article that a group of advocates came together to express concerns about this issue, stating that "they felt that the patient has made the choice to ingest the medicine and then our staff just walks away." Zatulovsky went on to say that "this was not aligned with our values of offering hope and care to our patients, so we changed our policy."[30]

Self-Administered versus Clinician-Administered Aid in Dying

In Canada, medical assistance in dying (which Canadians refer to as MAiD) is practiced much differently than it is in the United States. Canada is one of only four places in the world—along with Belgium, the Netherlands, and Luxembourg—where patients can choose self-administered medical assistance (similar to how it is practiced in the United States) or clinician-administered medical assistance in dying—which means a physician or nurse practitioner can administer drugs intravenously to aid patients in their death.

To even be considered eligible for MAiD under Canadian Bill C-14 (passed in 2016), a patient must be at least eighteen years old, have made a written request in front of two witnesses, and must be fully capable of making medical decisions. In order to be granted a request, two separate clinicians (only after a ten-day waiting period following submission of the written request) must determine that the patient has a "grievous and irremediable medical condition" that causes the person "enduring and intolerable suffering."[31] Importantly, a "grievous and irremediable medical condition" does *not* necessarily mean that a person has six or fewer months to live but rather is defined in subsection 241.2(2) of the bill as:

- having a serious and incurable illness, disease or disability; and,

- being in an advanced state of irreversible decline in capability; and,

- experiencing enduring physical or psychological suffering, due to the illness, disease, disability or state of decline, that is intolerable to the person and cannot be relieved in a manner that they consider acceptable; and,

- [anticipating that] where the person's natural death has become reasonably foreseeable taking into account all of their medical circumstances, without requiring a specific prognosis as to the length of time the person has left to live.

Two and a half years after the bill was enacted, it was estimated that 1.5 percent of the deaths in Canada were by medical assisted dying.[32] Interestingly, like some patients in the United States who qualify for physician aid in dying but who do not end up taking the life-ending prescription, not all Canadians who request MAiD follow through with their decision. It seems that for those who qualify for it, the reassurance of MAiD as an option is therapeutic in and of itself, offering them a sense of control over their suffering, even if they don't choose to end their suffering with the assistance of a clinician.

Speaking to this point during a presentation to the Hemlock Society of San Diego, physician Stefanie Green, cofounder and president of the Canadian Association for MAiD, described the moment when she is able to tell patients that they have qualified for MAiD:

Of all the things I do, I love that moment the most. Because when I tell a patient they are now able to have an assisted death if they want one, it's probably the most therapeutic thing I can do. Immediately their suffering goes down; immediately they feel empowered. And it doesn't matter what happens after that, to some extent. They already feel better; they're going to do better. And if they die of a natural cause, they almost don't care anymore because they now know that they can do this. It's very, very satisfying to them, and I love that.[33]

For some health care professionals, however, offering comprehensive hospice care is preferred over aid in dying. In fact, when patients request aid in dying in the United States, physicians must ask them if they understand their end-of-life options, including hospice care. Experts suggest that patients seeking aid in dying who aren't enrolled in hospice should be enrolled before being granted a request for aid, given the other options available to them.[34] After enrolling in hospice, for instance, some patients with significant and uncontrollable symptoms, such as extreme pain, delirium, difficulty breathing, and unrelenting vomiting, might consider the option of palliative sedation. Palliative sedation, which is the controlled process of using medication to reduce a patient's consciousness—sometimes to the point of total unconsciousness—should be distinguished from aid in dying, given that the physician's intention is only to relieve refractory suffering rather than to cause the patient's death.[35] Undoubtedly, ethical issues along with personal, cultural, religious, and familial values complicate decisions about palliative sedation, especially because sedation can hasten death—though it should be noted that patients can live for days to weeks after being sedated, and sedation can be reversed. Indeed, one study showed that among the 186 patients who underwent palliative sedation to alleviate symptoms while at an inpatient palliative care unit, 23 percent were discharged to their homes alive.[36] Despite the fact that palliative sedation can limit patients' interactions with their friends and family as they die, many patients and their loved ones are relieved to know that palliative sedation is an option for them.[37] As an option of last resort after concerted efforts to relieve pain and suffering have failed, palliative sedation can offer patients and families a sense of agency in situations that feel frightening and out of control.

The hope for some health care professionals working in end-of-life care is that once patients hear about

all their options and receive the full-spectrum, supportive care that hospice offers, they will no longer feel the
need to pursue aid in dying. Nevertheless, there are patients approaching the end of life—even those who are
receiving excellent hospice care and presented with alternative options—whose suffering is extraordinary, both
physically and existentially. And for those patients who
live in places within the United States where they cannot
receive a prescription to end their life, some will choose
to voluntarily stop eating and drinking (VSED) in order to
hasten their death. While there is some ethical and legal
uncertainty surrounding VSED, it has been generally argued that because all patients have the right to decline
life-sustaining treatment, patients with a terminal or incurable illness who still have decision-making capacity can
voluntarily choose to stop eating food and taking in any
liquids since both are necessary to sustain life.[38] As such,
physicians cannot disallow or overturn the decision of a
patient with a terminal illness to stop eating and drinking,
though a physician or health care organization may decide
to not actively participate in this action, ultimately choosing, for example, to not treat the symptoms that arise
from VSED, such as pain or delirium. In such situations,
patients who want VSED might choose to find another
clinician or organization willing to support their decision,
or some patients and their families may choose to follow

through with the decision at home without any help from medical professionals.

Needless to say, care for the dying has changed significantly in Western society in the past sixty years, though disagreement persists about practitioners' role in actively hastening death, especially in the United States. Indeed, for some physicians, particularly those significantly shaped by a training that is so focused on fixing, curing, and biological interventions, aiding patients in their death is seen as a total dereliction of their duty to save lives. And for others who might not feel morally opposed, they may still be hesitant to participate in aid in dying, since the idea of stepping into the metaphysical realm of life and death by helping patients end their lives may feel a bit too much like "playing God."

Regardless of practitioners' personal feelings, convictions, or misgivings about aid in dying, the fact remains that there are many patients who, fearing that their medical practitioners will not be able to adequately address their pain and suffering, want to ensure that their lives end on their own terms. While neither Shawn nor I participate in aid in dying (nor is it legal in our state), we do understand why patients might want to have control over the end of their lives given their doubts about whether their medical professionals will be there to address their total pain—the physical and existential suffering that comes with facing the end. Because of powerful political and systemic forces

Our fear is that when it comes to US medicine, there still remains no place for dying.

at both the micro- and macrolevels (which will be explored in the following chapters), we can see why patients might not trust that their doctors can treat total pain, or even recognize total pain when they see it. As such, we wonder whether hospice and palliative medicine have been able to offer the kind of care they've always intended to or whether they've made much of an impact on the broader culture of mainstream medicine—a culture that is still so preoccupied with treatments and fixes and biological interventions. Our fear is that when it comes to US medicine, there still remains no place for dying.

WHEN HOSPICE AND PALLIATIVE CARE ARE NOT ENOUGH

To Ivan Ilych only one question was important: was his case serious or not? But the doctor ignored that inappropriate question. From his point of view it was not the one under consideration, the real question was to decide between a floating kidney, chronic catarrh, or appendicitis.

—Leo Tolstoy, *The Death of Ivan Illych*

The world of modern medicine is massive, complex, and expansive. And yet despite its size and complexities, the way people die within that world has changed little over the past few decades. In our day-to-day work, Shawn and I often see patients and practitioners pursuing ineffective and aggressive treatment at the end of life, with both sides sometimes unsure of how they got there in the first place. Indeed, the path-dependent nature of modern medicine almost imperceptibly leads patients, families, and practitioners in the direction of active intervention, even when those interventions cause more suffering in the end.

Some may wonder, then, whether the efforts to transform end-of-life care have done much to transform the health care system as a whole or shift medicine's focus toward caring for the whole patient rather than trying to cure at all costs, which was one of the primary goals of the hospice movement nearly fifty years ago.[1] In other words, the question remains about whether the hospice movement made a significant impact on the broader culture of modern medicine, the culture that Shawn and his colleagues practice in every day, the culture my mom died within, and the culture my dad was entering when we started writing this book.

Watching Shawn work in that culture was one of the reasons I knew we needed to get my dad connected to a palliative care team after his diagnosis of stage-four gastric cancer. But when we'd asked his oncology clinic if there was a palliative medicine specialist on its team, we were told that the oncologists practiced their own palliative care, treating pain and symptoms as they arise. While I was glad to hear that the oncologists felt comfortable treating their patients' pain and symptoms, I was concerned that they wouldn't be able to both manage my dad's cancer treatment plan and address his complicated symptoms, like difficulty swallowing, anxiety, and sleepless nights, within their short fifteen-minute clinic visits. The current state of our health care system, largely defined by short visits and high throughput, didn't seem like it would allow his oncologists enough time to do the complicated, highly specialized work they do while also addressing my dad's total pain. I worried that there wouldn't be enough time to have the rather lengthy conversations about goals for my dad's care that would ensure his treatment plan was aligned with his values—conversations that those in palliative medicine are so good at having. And I was worried that important conversations about when to stop treatment and focus on comfort and quality of life would happen too late—just like they had with my mom—or worse, not happen at all. Nevertheless, we followed the oncologists' lead when it came to addressing my dad's symptoms, for at least a little while.

About four months after my dad's diagnosis, Shawn started a monthlong training in the ICU. I vividly remember when he called me on his way home after one of his first shifts to tell me about a forty-five-year-old patient they'd tried to resuscitate in front of his wife and teenage son, and how none of them—not the patient or his family—seemed to understand how sick the man was. The patient had been diagnosed with stage-four lung cancer a few months prior, and when he showed up to the ED with his wife and son because he was having difficulty breathing, it was clear that no one had talked to him or his family about the fact that his cancer was ultimately terminal and his death was near. As a result, the patient and his family (quite understandably) insisted the medical team do anything necessary to fix what was wrong, without understanding that the underlying problem could not be fixed: the man was struggling to breathe because he was actively dying of cancer.

Shawn said the whole experience reminded him of a story that physician Atul Gawande recounts in his book *Being Mortal* about one of his patients, Mr. Lazaroff, who chose to pursue an aggressive surgical procedure near the end of his life. While the surgery was a technical success (the surgical team was able to remove the mass invading Mr. Lazaroff's spine), it did not cure his cancer, extend his life, or even improve the quality of the life he had left. In fact, Mr. Lazaroff never recovered from the procedure. He died in the hospital after spending his last days on a ventilator.

Perhaps the most unsettling part of the story is that Mr. Lazaroff went down this path in part because his care team never honestly addressed how sick he was. As Gawande puts it,

> We had no difficulty explaining the specific dangers of various treatment options, but we never really touched on the reality of his disease. His oncologists,

radiation therapists, surgeons and other doctors had all seen him through months of treatments for a problem that they knew could not be cured. We could never bring ourselves to discuss the larger truth about his condition or the ultimate limits of our capabilities, let alone what might matter most to him as he neared the end of his life. If he was pursuing a delusion, so were we.[2]

Similarly, Shawn was horrified that no one seemed to have ever talked honestly and directly to his patient in the ICU about how sick he was, what to expect as his illness progressed, and whether he wanted to spend his final moments at home or in the ICU as his wife and son watched him die attached to a machine giving him mechanical chest compressions. Rather, these conversations occurred too late, when he was already in crisis, when "doing everything" seemed like the only possible choice to make in an emergency situation the patient and his family never saw coming. Shawn said the worst part was seeing the obvious fear and horror on the man's face increase with every passing minute as he struggled for air, knowing that he could not change the fact that this man was dying. While he knew he could treat the man's symptoms and provide some comfort, Shawn was instead being asked to perform CPR and insert a tube in the man's throat, inevitably increasing both his and his family's suffering.

When Shawn told me about how this patient died— how his wife and son seemed totally traumatized by the whole event—I couldn't help but think of my dad and hope the end would not look like that for him. I worried that without *active* intervention from Shawn or me, or without connecting my dad to a palliative care team, this was the kind of end he'd inevitably experience. Without intentionally changing directions, it seemed like this was just the natural path that medicine paved for him—for so many patients—despite the noble efforts of the hospice movement over the past four decades.

While it is true that more patients are receiving hospice care at the end of life and fewer patients are dying in the hospital, when you take a closer look at the data, you can see that many of these patients are entering hospice just days before they die, which means they still might've spent much of their final days and weeks in the hospital, even if they were discharged in time to die elsewhere. In 2016, for instance, nearly 30 percent of the patients who were fortunate enough to be enrolled in hospice died within seven days, with some of them dying within one day of enrolling.[3] So while less people are physically dying within the walls of the hospital, they may not be spending less time as patients in the hospital before they die.

Take Arizona, for example, where we live and where over 70 percent of dying patients who received a hospice referral in 2018 were referred in the last thirty days of life.[4] Among these patients, 38 percent of those who died of cancer had an ICU stay in the last thirty days of their lives, and 61 percent spent time in the ED. Add to this the fact that 82 percent of these cancer patients had *more than ten* medical providers in the last six months of life, and it is safe to assume that these patients were unlikely receiving streamlined care focused on quality of life. To the contrary, the last few months of most of these patients' lives likely looked similar to my mother's: driving to countless doctors' appointments; enduring treatments, scans, procedures, and even surgeries; and living in general confusion about a plan of care, especially when numerous physicians caring for the same person are not coordinating their efforts.

Late referrals to hospice not only affect quality of life for patients but also their loved ones. Families of patients with late referrals to hospice have reported lower satisfaction with hospice services, a higher rate of unmet needs for information about what to expect at the time of death, lower confidence in caring for their loved one at home, and more concerns with coordination of care.[5] Concerns about coordinating care are intensified for terminally ill patients and their families who belong to lower socioeconomic groups. Hospice's focus on in-home care can limit services to only those patients who have family members or friends in the home to provide that care. As such, patients who live alone or those from low-income households where family members cannot afford to leave work to be with them may not receive adequate care when they need it most.[6] While hospice organizations do attempt to offer inpatient care at a hospice facility or skilled nursing facility for those patients who do not have anyone at home to care for them, it can be difficult for hospice agencies to justify inpatient stays for these patients, especially in recent years as the Centers for Medicare and Medicaid Services (CMS) have tightened their regulations around general inpatient (GIP) care for hospice patients. These tighter regulations have been, in part, a response to a 2016 report published by the US Department of Health and Human Services Office of Inspector General that claimed hospices were inappropriately billing Medicare for GIP care for patients who did not meet the GIP criteria (only patients who need specialized procedures or symptom management that cannot be feasibly provided in another setting qualify for GIP).[7] CMS agreed with the recommendations of the report and subsequently expanded its oversight of GIP claims and increased its surveyor efforts.

While there is and always will be a need for regulations and oversight in order to prevent fraudulent behavior and ensure quality care for patients, the effort to reduce "inappropriate" GIP stays and discharge patients sooner (or deny them inpatient stays altogether) appears to be frequently aimed at reducing costs and rarely aligned with patients' best interests. Our colleagues and mentors who have practiced end-of-life care long enough to see the consequences of such policy changes over the years have expressed concern that increased regulation disproportionately affects their most vulnerable patients. For patients without significant financial resources or without loved ones to provide caregiver support in the home, tighter regulations around GIP admission and length of stay have made it increasingly more difficult to find a place for them to safely spend their final weeks or days of life.

Clearly, disparities in access to and quality of end-of-life care exist among economically disadvantaged groups, but they also exist among racial minorities, regardless of their socioeconomic status. Data from 2017, for instance, show that 49 percent of white patients died while under the care of hospice compared with only 36 percent of black patients.[8] And a 2016 study suggests that even when black patients are enrolled in hospice, they have worse outcomes than white patients, regardless of things like income, education, socioeconomic status, gender, marital status, and religiosity.[9] The study showed that these patients were significantly more likely than white patients who were enrolled in hospice to be admitted to the hospital (14.9 versus 8.7 percent), go to the emergency room (19.8 versus 13.5 percent), and disenroll from hospice prior to death (18.1 versus 13.0 percent).

This is not to say that the hospice movement and standards for end-of-life care that arose from it are things to be dismissed. Quite the opposite: the hospice movement and changes in care for the dying that came from it are invaluable—more patients are dying where and how they'd prefer to die, and those in medicine are more aware of the needs of the dying. And the families who have benefited from hospice services can attest to the compassionate care and transformative experiences hospice care can provide. Nevertheless, the problems that plague end-of-life care—including disparities in access to health care as well as the broader culture of medicine that is still so dominated by productivity, efficiency, fragmented care, and an emphasis on cure—cannot be remedied by the introduction of hospice and palliative care alone.

Who's Having the Hard Conversations?

Precisely because the introduction of hospice care in the 1970s and then palliative medicine thirty years later has not been enough to change the culture of mainstream medicine, Shawn and I were not surprised when it finally became clear that my dad's symptoms, worries, and fears were not being addressed adequately during his visits with his oncologists and primary care doctor. As my dad's symptoms began to progress about six months after his diagnosis, Shawn and I talked to him about enrolling in a new program in our city that offered home palliative care services for patients who were still receiving cancer

The problems that plague end-of-life care cannot be remedied by the introduction of hospice and palliative care alone.

treatment and were not yet ready to enroll in hospice. My dad said that an extra set of eyes on him wouldn't be a bad idea. So it wasn't long before we arranged a meeting at his house with a palliative medicine physician.

During that meeting, the doctor explained to us that a nurse would be available to my dad by phone twenty-four hours a day in order to address any concerns that came up over the next few months. He also said the nurse could come directly to the house if my dad needed anything urgently and that she would be coming out weekly to check up on him. The doctor then went through every one of my dad's medications—and there were a lot—and eliminated the ones that my dad had been taking for years that were likely not benefiting him anymore, given the drastic changes in his body over the last few months. He then spent some time talking to my dad about what his hopes were for the chemotherapy treatment he was receiving, to which my dad responded that he hoped it would shrink the tumor in his stomach so that he'd be able to eat without too much trouble and then have enough energy to get out of the house from time to time. His doctor said he hoped for that too and would do whatever he could to help my dad get his strength back so that his life could feel at least a little more like normal.

Finally, the doctor asked if my dad had given any thought to when he'd know he'd had enough, when he'd know that the side effects of the treatments weren't worth it anymore. To that, my dad said that he hadn't given it much thought, that right now he still wanted to get treatment and wanted to focus on those treatments for the next few months. The doctor said that sounded like a fine plan and if anything changed, my dad could call him to talk about it, or he'd come over and see him, and they'd come up with a new plan together—that he'd help him understand his options if and when decisions needed to be made.

I was so grateful for this visit. I was grateful that this doctor had at least started some of the inevitable—and really hard—conversations that we'd need to have more frequently as time progressed. I was grateful that he'd listened to my dad about which of his symptoms caused him the most distress, pared down the amount of pills my dad took each day, and let my dad cry when he said how badly he wanted to "feel normal" again. Most of all, I was grateful to feel less alone in navigating the path of my dad's medical journey.

And yet I was bewildered by the fact that we felt alone on the journey at all given that Shawn and I both work in health care and should've known how to navigate things ourselves. I wondered why my dad's path until that point had seemed so unclear. I wondered why the kind of conversation the doctor had with my dad could not have happened sooner, why it couldn't have happened with any of the other four or five doctors who were taking care of him. Why did it feel like only the palliative medicine team could or should have a conversation with my dad about his current quality of life as well as his goals for medical treatment?

I recently posed this question to one of my colleagues who was a hospice nurse for three years before she became a nurse practitioner in oncology who cares for patients at a cancer clinic in the Midwest. I asked her what her experience is like caring for her patients with cancer and whether she sees her nurse practitioner and physician colleagues having these hard conversations about patients' hopes and goals of care. She replied,

> There are certain cancers that we can catch early and have pretty good outcomes after treatment. So those conversations look different. They're less scary and more hopeful. But it's a different story when patients have advanced cancers. When it comes down to it, we don't talk about reality soon enough with these patients. We don't talk about whether they want to live two or three more weeks getting treatment in the hospital, or one week more at home with their family. People care about the way they die. But that conversation is just so hard.

These conversations certainly are hard. In fact, they were so hard for my mom and me that we never even had them. And they were still hard years later with my dad, despite the fact that I knew what would happen if we avoided them. But what I have come to see over the years is that these conversations are not just hard for patients and their families. They are also difficult for the doctors and health care professionals who care for them, as my colleague pointed out. Confronting human mortality is uncomfortable, and some philosophers and scholars argue that all of us share a deep anxiety about death and finitude—an anxiety that makes conversations that force us to face our mortality exceedingly difficult to engage in.[10]

Death Anxiety

For centuries, philosophers have asserted that our anxiety about death is existential, meaning that it's part of the human condition we can never escape, even if there are some cultural traditions and religious practices that can mitigate some of that anxiety.[11] Over two thousand years ago, Greek philosopher Epicurus said that the root cause of human misery is our omnipresent fear of inevitable death. Drawing on Epicurus's writings, contemporary psychologist Irvin Yalom argues that nearly all our emotional and psychological struggles can be traced back to our deep anxieties about death. According to Yalom, this fear is so pervasive that we "generate methods to soften death's terror. . . . [W]e project ourselves into the future through our children, grow rich, famous, ever larger; we develop compulsive protective rituals; or we embrace an impregnable belief in an ultimate rescuer."[12]

Yalom's contention is similar to that of US anthropologist Ernest Becker, who suggested in his 1973 book *The Denial of Death* that our most basic human drive is not rooted in sexuality or aggression, as Sigmund Freud had asserted, but rather in the terror produced in a (human) being that has attained self-awareness and knows that they will die.[13] In other words, the conscious and unconscious motivation for virtually all human behavior is the need to control or deny our basic anxiety: the terror of death and our undeniable mortality. In the foreword to Becker's text, Sam Keen writes,

> Elisabeth Kübler-Ross and Ernest Becker were strange allies in fomenting the cultural revolution that brought death and dying out of the closet. At the same time that Kübler-Ross gave us permission to practice the art of dying gracefully, Becker taught us that awe, fear, and ontological anxiety were natural accompaniments to our contemplation of the fact of death.[14]

Death Anxiety and Medicine

It is this particular conception of death anxiety that has led others to make similar claims about the death-fearing culture of the West and its relationship with modern medicine. Physician and philosopher Jeffrey Bishop, for instance, in his 2011 book *The Anticipatory Corpse*, goes as far as saying that death is the "repressed core" of both Western culture and the culture of medicine. As a result of this repression, humanity "dreams the dream of eternal life, health, and youth," and turns to the medical enterprise to make this dream a reality—"an enterprise that keeps aiming at eternity precisely because of the sting of death."[15] From Bishop's perspective, it is not only patients who approach medicine with this expectation but also practitioners who fail to see that many of their biological interventions simply cover over deeper questions about mortality and perpetuate unrealistic expectations for bodily restoration and cure.

Likewise, physician and author Sherwin Nuland claims that physicians not only have their own psychological qualms and anxieties about death but also personalities that are defined by a fear of failure along with a desire for control and certainty, which can contribute to a tendency to "indulge a very sick person and himself in a form of medical 'doing something' to deny the hovering presence of death" rather than helping patients confront the reality of their situations.[16] Nuland's argument is supported by studies from the 1960s that suggest physicians have greater death anxiety and are more fearful of death compared to patients as well as people who are not sick.[17] Herman Feifel and his colleagues, for example, conducted qualitative interviews in the late 1960s that revealed increased death anxiety among surgeons, internists, and psychiatrists. The researchers concluded that an elevated fear of death might be a reason for choosing medicine as a career in the first place.[18] Perhaps those with more death anxiety, they proposed, would be drawn to a career that is oriented toward controlling death and dying.[19]

Other research indicates that increased death anxiety among doctors might prevent them from having difficult conversations about diagnoses and prognoses with their patients, or even lead them to avoid suffering patients altogether.[20] In a study that looked at the psychological responses of medical staff caring for patients in oncology departments, Sandra Kocijan Lovko and her colleagues found that compared to staff working on general medicine floors, those in oncology more often emotionally distance themselves from seriously ill or dying patients as a form of self-protection.[21] One way clinicians do this is by focusing only on the physical management of symptoms, like pain control, rather than the emotional realities of suffering. As psychiatrist Peter Maguire notes in his research on the barriers to quality care for the dying, some of those providing medical care to terminal patients acknowledge that their emphasis on pain control and physical symptom relief could "be the most effective distancing tactic of all."[22]

Taken together, such research indicates that increased death anxiety among some clinicians can manifest itself in the desire to control illness and death, focus on the biological aspects of illness only, or avoid dying patients altogether. As a result, mainstream medicine has a strange relationship with death—one that acknowledges death as a biological phenomenon that ought to be controlled via medical intervention and simultaneously denies death as an existential reality. This kind of relationship is sustained by (and also creates) clinicians who approach and manage death as a biological event, while at the same time distancing themselves from the idea of death as an inevitable reality—a reality not only for their patients but also for themselves.[23]

And yet it's understandable why some clinicians avoid these conversations. Confronting the vulnerability of patients reminds them of their own mortality, and few people are comfortable sitting with this vulnerability for too long. Add to this the emotions that such conversations can evoke from patients and their families, and it makes sense that physicians might choose to narrow their conversations to treatment plans and symptom management. My colleague practicing in the Midwest, for example, told me about experiences she's had where she spent time talking to a patient and their family about transitioning to comfort care after chemotherapy treatments were no longer working, only to get a phone call later from the oncologist, who was ready to "try just one other thing":

> And then I think to myself—if that was me, I wouldn't want the other thing. I would want to be home with my family. I don't want the treatment that's just going to make things worse, you know? I think some physicians have a hard time letting go of steering the ship. They have a really hard time letting palliative care in. Which is such a shame because palliative care should be consulted early. The palliative team talks about what matters. Some of the oncologists I used to work with talked mostly about treatment. They talked about, "What are we going to do in this moment to prolong your life?" without talking about what exactly prolonging your life might look like in the end.

The Paradox of Palliative Care

My colleague's assessment that we need more physicians who are comfortable with helping patients transition their care from an emphasis on treatment toward an emphasis on quality and comfort when those treatments are no longer providing any benefit seems right to me, as does her suggestion that we need more physicians who are willing to consult the palliative care team. To some, it may seem strange that physicians aren't *more* eager to consult a palliative care team given the extra support, care, and coordination they provide for their patients, but there are reasons why physicians are not eager to seek out a consult. While a resistance to having emotional conversations that evoke feelings of anxiety (for both patients and doctors) likely contributes to their hesitation, there are also systemic issues endemic to our health care system that discourage the initiation of palliative care.

Take, for instance, a universal outcome measure included in databases used by hospitals, governmental agencies, professional societies, and researchers called "operative mortality." Operative mortality is just what it sounds like: deaths that occur after an operation. More specifically, it is traditionally defined as any death, regardless of cause, occurring *within* thirty days after surgery (in or out of the hospital) or *after* thirty days but during the same hospitalization subsequent to the operation.[24] Outcome measures like these can discourage surgeons from consulting the palliative care team early on during a hospital stay, even for the sickest and most complex patients, out of fear that the palliative team might "let the patient die" within the thirty-day window. As one of my palliative care colleagues who works in another state recently said to me, "You'd be shocked by how many consults we get on day thirty-one of a patient's hospital stay." On day thirty-one, a patient can be transferred to a skilled nursing facility or go home on hospice care, die outside the walls of the hospital, and therefore not "count" as an operative mortality.

There are more shocking, but fortunately rarer, instances of avoiding palliative care consults in order to keep patients alive for the sake of survival rates. Recently, *Pro-Publica* released an article describing its investigation of Newark Beth Israel Medical Center. The piece uncovered that the hospital had apparently tailored the care of at least four patients who received transplants in order to keep them alive to boost survival rates.[25] Because the Scientific Registry of Transplant Recipients—which tracks and analyzes transplant outcomes for the US government—monitors the survival rates of heart transplant patients based on those who live for one year posttransplant, the hospital's transplant program was apparently worried about being penalized or losing funding based on its one-year survival rates (84.2 percent), which were below the national average (91.5 percent). In a recording of a clinical team meeting obtained by *ProPublica*, doctors were overheard discussing their plan to keep a patient, who had been in an unresponsive state for months, on life support so that they would not have to report the death and put the transplant program's funding in jeopardy. According to the article, the recording reveals one of the doctors cautioning the staff against offering the patient's family the option of switching from aggressive treatment to palliative care until reaching the one-year mark of the patient's transplant. In the recording, the director of the hospital's heart and lung transplant programs is overheard saying that they "need to keep [the patient] alive until June 30th at a minimum," before another physician asks whether the patient's family had requested that the team withdraw care. To this, the director responded, "We haven't refused anything they've asked. . . . We just haven't raised withdrawing it."[26]

Undoubtedly there are many complex—and sometimes deeply disturbing—reasons why a palliative care consult comes too late or never comes at all. But perhaps the biggest reason, and the one that is most difficult to address, is the larger culture of contemporary medicine that has yet to consider the care for the dying as the responsibility of all health care practitioners. The current paradigm of US medicine tends to isolate the two "spheres" of curative and palliative care, and as such, the kind of care offered by hospice and palliative teams is still perceived as something wholly separate from the dominant curative sphere of medicine. As a result, physicians who identify with the curative sphere may feel that caring for dying patients is not their responsibility and therefore simply "hand off" their patients to a palliative team.[27]

Our fear is that the introduction of palliative medicine as a medical specialty has unintentionally and paradoxically widened the gap between these curative and palliative spheres of patient care, leaving some physicians to assume that care for the dying is "not their job" and "better left to the experts." I have heard countless stories from palliative medicine doctors, nurse practitioners, and social workers who are asked to come in at the eleventh hour to discuss code status or the withdrawal of treatment with dying patients or their families at the end of a long hospital stay. These practitioners express disappointment that their physician colleagues were unwilling to have these conversations with their patients themselves—and have them much earlier. Instead, patients are left having these conversations with a group of well-intentioned strangers at the end of their illness trajectory, just like my mother did, rather than with their primary physician or surgeon, with whom they may have a long-standing relationship. It's not surprising, then, that some patients can feel abandoned when they are handed off to a palliative care team when curative treatments are no longer an option, rarely—if ever—seeing their primary physician again.

So while the introduction of hospice care and palliative medicine has made those who practice medicine more aware of the care that is available to those with chronic or terminal illness, and has brought these resources closer to practitioners, it also may have inadvertently distanced clinicians from the work itself. Just recently I was speaking to my coworker—a family medicine physician of many years—about this phenomenon. He told me that fifteen or twenty years ago, he cared for all his patients "from cradle to grave" and provided palliative care himself for his patients with complex or terminal illnesses. "I've noticed a difference since palliative medicine has become a specialty," he told me. "You get the feeling in the hospital that you're supposed to consult the specialist in order to manage your patient's pain or other physical and emotional symptoms, rather than managing these things yourself."

The Need for Primary Palliative Care

For these reasons, leaders in palliative care have made it clear that they believe all physicians ought to be providing palliative care and have started to distinguish between "specialty" and "nonspecialty" (or "primary") palliative care. The Institute of Medicine defines specialty palliative care as that which is "delivered by health care professionals who are palliative care specialists, such as physicians who are board certified in this specialty; palliative-certified nurses; and palliative care-certified social workers, pharmacists, and chaplains," while primary palliative care is "delivered by health care professionals who are *not* palliative care specialists, such as primary care clinicians; physicians who are disease-oriented specialists (such as oncologists and cardiologists); and nurses, social workers, pharmacists, chaplains, and others who care for this population but are not certified in palliative care."[28]

The purpose of this distinction between primary and specialty palliative care is to encourage *all* medical professionals—not just palliative care "experts"—to attend to the physical, emotional, and existential elements of pain and suffering by offering primary palliative care. In this respect, all physicians, regardless of medical specialty, are called to practice palliative care and provide it at the beginning of the illness trajectory, alongside curative treatment. Primary palliative care should be offered often and early, and specialty palliative care services should be reserved for those patients with intractable pain or particularly complex symptoms like my dad, or for those who are ready to transition to hospice care (which is itself "specialized" palliative care for those closer to the end of life). My dad, for example, was receiving "specialty" palliative care from the team that was coming to his home to address his complicated symptoms that had not been adequately addressed by his other care team.

While these important distinctions have been made within the field of palliative medicine, encouraging all physicians to see palliative care as part of their everyday practice is going to take time and will require a total paradigm shift within both medical training and practice. It will require the sphere of palliative medicine to intersect deeply and meaningfully with the curative sphere of mainstream medicine. This move, however, is exceedingly difficult in a medical system so defined by specialized care, in which many medical experts tend to focus on the care of one or two organ systems, rather than care of the whole person and their overall treatment trajectory. Nevertheless, helping practitioners keep an eye on a patient's overall well-being and the long-term goals of care is critical for shifting the culture of mainstream medicine.

Some might argue that such a shift, if successful, would render the specialty of palliative medicine totally obsolete. Yet this seems unlikely given that the work of palliative medicine specialists would still be needed for pain and suffering that is difficult to treat and requires expert care. And it should go without saying that if palliative medicine ceased to exist as a specialty because all physicians began addressing their patients' physical, emotional, social, and existential needs from diagnosis until death, the occasion likely would be met with celebration, not disappointment.

There are, however, critics of palliative medicine who argue that in its efforts to legitimize itself as a proper (read: scientific, rigorous, and evidence-based) medical specialty, it has lost its critical edge that once demanded a different kind of care for all patients, ultimately succumbing to the forces of mainstream medicine. As Bishop puts it,

It appears, at first, that in palliative care the caregivers offer themselves as companions to the dying. But for the sake of appearing scientific . . . palliative medicine deploys tools of assessment to refine not only its care of the patient and family but also to justify its own functioning. It becomes a set of expert discourses intended to prove its own value in the care of the dying. It cloaks death in its own definitions and assessments and interventions.[29]

The Latin root of "palliative" is *pallio*, meaning to disguise or cloak, and for Bishop the term is fitting; palliative medicine's efforts to legitimize its existence simply cover over the human being who suffers beneath these efforts.[30] That is, with all their "expertise" and interventions—treating pain, completing documents, and managing physical symptoms—palliative medicine specialists not only fail to see the everyday experience of patients, including the ways they suffer existentially, but also fail to act as the patient's companion in that experience.

Palliative and Hospice Care: Do They Always Lead to a "Good Death"?

Like Bishop, other clinicians and scholars are critical of the perceived encroachment of hospice and palliative care on society's understanding of a good death. As sociologist Bethne Hart and her colleagues point out, the ideology of the good death may actually serve to prescribe "socially approved" or normalized forms of death and dying, which include coming to terms with one's finitude, passively accepting death, and dying in physical and emotional comfort. As they observe,

> We have "good deaths" and "bad deaths" and "good" and "bad" patients; these stereotypes recur within hospital and hospice care. Sociological, psychological, and nursing research has already demonstrated . . . that "bad" patients are those who fail to conform, who deviate from normative behaviors and choices, and who fail to legitimate the role of their caregivers.[31]

Such an emphasis on a good death can cause some to assume that patients who choose to "fight" their disease to the end via treatments and procedures, or those who face their death with anger and outrage, inevitably experience a bad death. Sandra Gilbert, author of *Death's Door: Modern Dying and the Ways We Grieve*, has argued that "Death with Dignity"—the motto of hospice advocates and other followers of Kübler-Ross—does not allow for "ways of meeting death with indignation—or at least of challenging the indignity of death itself." As she sees it, the insistence on a peaceful and pain-free death at home may actually serve as a strategy to "contain" the "rage and fear that aren't all that different from the many other depersonalizing techniques of the hospital itself."[32] Prescribing good ways of dying, then, can be just as impersonal and constrictive as a medicalized hospital death. And for families, not providing a so-called good death for their loved one—because their loved one dies in the hospital, for instance—can leave them feeling guilt or shame for having somehow "failed" to offer a good death at home.

Fortunately, leaders within contemporary hospice and palliative care have nuanced their descriptions of the good death, even going as far as saying that there "is no one good death," and end-of-life experiences should be "negotiated and renegotiated in the context of that patient's and family's values, preferences, and life course."[33] This nuanced perspective is critical given the huge variation of preferences and values among patients—values and preferences that are significantly shaped by culture, ethnicity, religion, and identity.[34]

Dying at Home: The Invisible Death Returns

In talking to some of my medical students and residents about good and bad deaths, I've come to see how few of them have real experiences with the dying process and helping patients die well throughout that process. This seems to be a result of the fact that they rarely "see" deaths in the hospital at all—or more specifically, they rarely see *dying* in the hospital. Of course, they see when patients code or die in the ICU after they are removed from supportive measures like ventilators, but they rarely see patients die the way my mom did, or the way so many patients do at the end of prolonged chronic or terminal illnesses. As my medical student, Rob, explained to me when I asked him about his experiences caring for patients at the end of life,

> It's strange because I don't actually see any of them die. Well, I mean, I've seen a lot of patients die, but they kind of die instantly after a code or after we extubate them. But I haven't really helped anyone die for days or weeks or something, after they decide they want to stop treatments. They're just sort of gone, out of the hospital, after they make that decision. So it's like death is happening all the time in medicine, but I'm not actually *experiencing* it.

Medical trainees like Rob have to intentionally seek out opportunities with hospice and palliative care teams in order to see the natural dying process since this happens so infrequently in the hospital. And this may help explain why I felt so uncomfortable while my mom was dying in the hospital, like we weren't "supposed" to be there, like we were in the way. Death, dying, and grief feel out of place in the fast-paced and "professionally" detached world of the hospital. As Ariès put it, "When death arrives . . . it must not interrupt the hospital routine, which is more delicate than that of any other professional milieu."[35] And like Rob told me, "The structure of the hospital can really prevent you from connecting with patients, and when someone dies, you're so busy that you don't really have time to let it affect you."

Clearly, the hospital is not the place where many people want to die or should have to die, given that so few of the professionals who work there have the experience or training to support patients and families in navigating the process. Because of this, dying at home or in a hospice facility with professionals trained in end-of-life care seems like a much better alternative. And yet when patients are taken out of the hospital and moved into their homes or outside facilities, clinicians and trainees who work in the hospital do not see—let alone help with—the natural process of dying. One might wonder, then, if taking dying patients outside its walls contributes to the hospital's inability to hold space for the realities of suffering, death, and loss, and simply bolsters the curative focus of mainstream medicine. Ariès argued that the hospital of the 1960s offered families a place to sequester the dying, to "hide the unseemly invalid whom neither the world nor they [could] endure."[36] Perhaps today's emphasis on dying *outside* the hospital serves a similar need for those who work there: to make death invisible, to render it obsolete in hospital medicine so that the institution can press on efficiently and clinicians do not have to confront the limits of their medical efforts in the face of human mortality.

Whether it occurs inside or outside a hospital's walls, death holds—and has always held—a strange place in the US hospital. Delaying death's arrival motivates nearly every move, and yet when death finally does appear, there are few who are willing to stand in its presence. And it is this difficulty with being present that makes the good death so elusive. When patients die in ways that are inconsistent with their wishes, it is often a result of others' inability to be present with them and allow them to express what they want in the end.

Regardless of whether patients want to seek treatment until the end or want to limit medical interventions and die at home, those who are called to care for patients should be able to be present during the journey and have the courage (and training) to help patients make important decisions along the way. A good death should be consistent with the narrative of patients' whole lives, even if this means dying in the hospital, *as long as that is what the patient wanted*. A hospital death should not be the default result of a hard conversation that never happened.

Patients—in conversation with their families and clinicians—ought to be able to determine what a good

Those who . . . care for patients should be present during the journey and have the courage (and training) to help patients make important decisions along the way.

death looks like for them. And data show us that some are better than others at being present for conversations that help patients make this determination. In Arizona, for example, nearly 70 percent of patients say that they have expressed their wishes for end-of-life care with their family members or loved ones, while only 18 percent of them have talked about their wishes with their doctor.[37] And a 2015 survey of the general public by the Kaiser Health Foundation found that while 89 percent of patients thought a discussion with their physician about end-of-life care choices was important, only 17 percent had actually had one.[38] This is a serious problem given that patients' care at the end of life can end up drastically different from their wishes when their physicians are not aware of their desires.

It's important to note that many patients believe it is their physician's responsibility to initiate end-of-life conversations.[39] While some might argue that patients should take initiative and bring up these topics with their doctors, this notion fails to consider the power dynamics inherent in patient-physician relationships. In my own experiences both professionally and personally, I have found that doctors' words are particularly weighty and significant, especially when it comes to diagnoses and prognoses. Because of this, and because physicians have specific training and expertise related to illness processes and outcomes, psychologists Richard McQuellon and Michael

Cowen contend that doctors are "rightfully expected to assume greater responsibility" for initiating and sustaining difficult conversations, particularly if they are about the prospect of death.[40]

Hospice and Palliative Care: Looking Forward

We believe that despite the criticism levied against their field, practitioners of hospice and palliative medicine—when they do not feel compelled to show their "worth" via the same metrics as mainstream medicine—can help patients live and die in ways that are consistent with their wishes and be present with them until the end of their journeys, while also working to shift the broader culture of medicine that has not yet assumed greater responsibility for having difficult conversations. Hospice and palliative medicine can do, and does, so much more than manage physical systems or provide support for patients, families, and other medical specialists. Indeed, physician Casey Sharpe argues that palliative medicine clinicians should resist the temptation to see themselves as merely providing an "extra layer of support" or to disproportionately emphasize the *measurable* outcomes of such support, regardless of its obvious benefits. Instead, practitioners should embrace what palliative medicine has always intended to do: walk alongside patients through the lived experience of serious illness and stand by them in their darkest times, triumphant moments, inevitable losses, and final farewells. As Sharpe sees it,

> There is no feature of serious illness more immediate or more essential than one's *lived experience* with that illness. . . . The notion that palliative care's most essential quality is incompatible with the highest standards of medical science has engendered an insecurity within our field—a concern that patients and clinicians alike, primed by the dominant epistemology of Western medicine, perceive little value added by palliative care. Due in part to this concern, our research and pedagogy have given disproportionate attention to quantitative knowledge of topics such as symptom management, measurable psychic outcomes, and prognostication. While such knowledge is important to the practice of palliative care, it is most often secondary to its central task of attending to lived experience.[41]

Sharpe goes on to say that when we overmedicalize palliative medicine's approach to patient care, the field risks "merely joining the parade of modern medicine rather than helping to lead it."[42] It's undeniable that the early hospice movement intended to transform care for the dying, and in many ways it has done so. But when it comes to leading the parade of modern medicine toward recognizing and attending to the lived experiences of illness and dying, the movement has fallen short.

Our hope, however, is that if contemporary hospice and palliative practice can resist being usurped by mainstream medical culture, it can return to leading the charge to help all practitioners engage in conversations with patients that are so needed, despite their difficulty and the existential anxiety they provoke within all of us. Rather than cloaking death, those who practice hospice and palliative medicine, when left unencumbered by the demands of modern medical culture, can unearth the fear and silence around death and begin to address the existential pain that mainstream medicine otherwise denies. Practiced in this way, "palliative" medicine is a misnomer given its focus on *uncovering* painful realities that when confronted directly, can be liberating for patients and those they love.

Hospice and palliative medicine should not shy away from promoting the kind of care it does best—coming alongside patients when they are most vulnerable—and should encourage all practitioners, in all specialties, to do the same. This is because one medical specialty on its own cannot change the kind of care patients receive at the end of life, as this care is not delivered in a vacuum. The forces that threaten hospice and palliative medicine's uniqueness by asking it to show its (economic) worth are the same forces that shape the way all patients live and die in the US health care system more broadly. They are the same forces that push for efficiency and productivity. They are the same forces that make it feel impossible for practitioners in other specialties to attend to the lived experience of illness when their appointments are hardly long enough to address physical symptoms. And they are the same forces that frame medicine as transactional, concealing the humanity of both patients and practitioners. Transforming care for those who are seriously ill or dying, then, requires larger shifts in the way care is delivered, especially in the United States, where perceived needs for productivity and profit determine the kind of care clinicians offer and patients receive.

THE BUSINESS OF DEATH

Any intelligent fool can make things bigger, more complex, and more violent. It takes a touch of genius, and a lot of courage, to move in the opposite direction.
—Albert Einstein

Hospice and palliative medicine exist within the larger health care system—a system that is generally homogeneous and monolithic. In many ways, the development of these medical specialties was a reaction to and attempted solution for some of the broader failings of that system. The most obvious of these failings is the curative focus of medicine that overlooks care for the dying. But the other less conspicuous "solution" that hospice and palliative medicine provide is the mitigation of health care costs in a country where nearly 18 percent of the gross domestic product—or $3 trillion a year—is spent on health care.

While hospice and palliative medicine embody a philosophy of care that has proven to lead to better outcomes as patients approach the end of life (for example, less invasive procedures along with fewer ICU stays and visits to the ED), in US medicine the value of these outcomes is reduced to just that: economic value. In a health care system grounded in an ethos of efficiency, productivity, and profit, hospice and palliative medicine have conveniently manifested as a patchwork fix to reduce the price associated with caring for patients at the end of life.

The Greatest Health Care in the World

There have been moments during my medical training and practice that have felt as if the United States has the best to offer when it comes to medical care: I've seen patients with catastrophic illnesses and injuries brought back from the brink, saved by innovative drugs, devices, and procedures. To be sure, if I ever experience a devastating injury or illness, or am in need of an elective, nonurgent procedure or surgery, I would hope to receive care in one of the many high-tech institutions in the US system. There is no doubt that our system is replete with advanced technology and some of the best-trained specialists in the world.

I am grateful that I'm privileged enough to have access to this health care system. And I am even more grateful that I've been fortunate enough to get the education and training necessary to participate in this system as a physician. I used to attribute my relative career success to the American dream, a rise from rags to riches where hard work allowed three generations of Abreus to go from a coal miner and carpenter, to a general contractor with a small construction business, and finally to me, a first-generation college graduate and the only doctor in both my immediate and extended family.

If, however, the American dream means living comfortably and having access to health care without the need for a college degree, then it was never ours for the taking. My all-American family, hardworking salt of the earth people—laborers, ranchers, and veterans—have never had consistent access to the US health care system, if they had access at all. All my life, my immediate family has lived paycheck to paycheck, insured only intermittently. As such, we constantly weighed seeing a doctor against the cost of doing so, and preventive care was a foreign concept. It's terrifying to look back at those times and realize that a catastrophic illness or injury experienced by my parents or any one of us five kids would have easily sent us into an unending cycle of extreme poverty. Fortunately this did not happen, and fortunately we always seemed to have friends in our school or church communities who could help us if we really needed it. Just a few years ago, during one of the many times she's been uninsured, my mother badly lacerated her foot after dropping a butcher's knife in the kitchen while cooking. Afraid of the bill from an urgent care or ED visit, she had her foot stitched by the veterinarian my parents know from their church.

To this day, my dad continues to make decisions about *which* of his diabetes medications he can afford to take at any one time rather than taking all the ones he needs, and my parents still risk periods of time without health insurance in order to keep up with the house payment. My parents' plight, however, is not uncommon, and there are millions of others who are much, much worse off than my family. I have met or worked with people who cannot afford dinner, much less a medical bill. And I have also seen people, like the woman I met in medical school with breast cancer, who only seek care when things become unbearable because they can't afford to see anyone sooner—and then die young because of it.

So how is it that we have the greatest, most expensive health care system in the world, and yet so many don't have access to it? The answer lies, in part, in what we define as "great." If greatness means having the most advanced options for fixing failing body parts, the US health care system is indeed the greatest. If greatness lies in generating profits for systems, insurers, and pharmaceutical and tech companies, we are unmatched. But if greatness means providing care to all who need it so that all (or any) of us live long, healthy lives and feel cared for from cradle to grave, then we are far, far from greatness.

Higher Costs for Better Health?

Reports suggest that US health care spending grew 4.6 percent in 2018, reaching $3.6 trillion.[1] We spend far more of our gross domestic product on health care per individual than does any other high-income country in the world. Trillions of dollars are difficult to fathom, so to put it into perspective, one might consider that the estimates of the cost for ending world hunger vary from $7 to $265 billion.[2] Taking even the highest of these estimates, we could end world hunger about thirteen times over with the price we pay for the US health care system. At the lower estimate, the figure is more than five hundred times over.

If we are investing, by far, the most money into our health care system compared to other high-income countries, we should be setting the bar worldwide for health and healthy living. The World Health Organization defines health as "a state of complete physical, mental, and social well-being and not merely the absence of disease or infirmity."[3] While some might contest this definition, seeing it as too broad and sweeping, most would agree that health means more than the absence of diagnosable disease. Indeed, many people who live with chronic disease and disability would still consider themselves healthy people with a good quality of life, despite the presence of illness or injury. Regardless of what one defines as "health" or "healthy," the question remains: Is the US health care system contributing to health more often than responding to disease?

Many would expect that an investment of over $3 trillion would yield far superior health outcomes in the United States compared to countries that spend less. Yet when comparing the United States with thirty-five similar countries, the United States experiences a higher infant mortality rate, higher prevalence of obesity, and lower life expectancy.[4] In the United States, life expectancy at birth is 78.6 years, ranking in the bottom quartile of life expectancy statistics in comparable, high-income countries, with the average person in the United States living about five fewer years than the average person living somewhere like Japan. What is more, many people on average in the United States are spending many of those 78.6 years in poor health. One metric, the Disability-Adjusted Life Year (DALY), measures how many years of healthy life were lost to illness, disability, or premature death; one DALY can be thought of as one lost year of "healthy" life.[5] The sum of these DALYs across the population measures the "disease burden" of a population, or the gap between current and ideal health, where an entire population would live to an advanced age, free of disease and disability. While disease burden has declined in the United States and comparable countries since 1990, the United States continues to have higher DALY rates than these other countries.[6] In 2015, for instance, the United States had an average rate of 23,104 healthy years lost per 100,000 people, while Sweden had an average rate of 17,749.[7]

While the mortality rates for breast, colorectal, and cervical cancers as well as the thirty-day mortality rate for heart attacks and ischemic stroke are lower in the United States than in comparable countries (for example, Germany, France, Switzerland, the United Kingdom, Australia, Sweden, Canada, and the Netherlands), the United States has higher mortality rates for respiratory, endocrine, nutritional, and metabolic diseases. Moreover, the US health care system has 37 percent higher rates of preventable hospital admissions for congestive heart failure, asthma, hypertension, and diabetes; higher rates of obstetric trauma for women during vaginal deliveries; and higher rates of medical, medication, or lab errors or delays (for instance, 19 percent of adults in the United States experience errors or delays, compared to 7 percent in Germany). And with the exception of Canada and Sweden, patients in the United States have a harder time making same-day appointments when in need of care than in other countries (for example, 51 percent of adults in the United States can make same-day appointments, compared to 77 percent in the Netherlands).[8] Not to mention, the United States has the highest rate of suicide relative to ten other high-income countries: Australia, Canada, France, Germany, the Netherlands, New Zealand, Norway, Sweden, Switzerland, and the United Kingdom.[9]

The bottom line is that people in the United States are not only living shorter lives but are also spending more of their lives sicker, more debilitated, and at increased risk for medical errors and delays in care compared to those who live in other high-income countries.

The Commodification of Medicine: Health Care and the Free Market

While the forces that lead to poorer health outcomes and shorter life spans among people in the United States are undeniably complex, the deeply pervasive and uniquely American commitment to the free market inevitably shapes the way health care is delivered and accessed in the United States. Basic principles of a free market system include competition, voluntary participation, transparency of information, and the determination of prices via the forces of supply and demand. When health care is considered a commodity like any other to be traded in the free market, it is believed that competition will result in a better product, since practitioners and researchers will

People in the United States are not only living shorter lives but are also spending more of their lives sicker and more debilitated.

compete with each other when it comes to quality, price, and consumer satisfaction in order to make a profit.[10] Patients, as "consumers," will then choose the best product for their needs based on price and quality, thereby encouraging price reduction and quality improvement.

In the world of medicine, Lasik eye surgery is often lauded as an example of the great success of free market principles in health care.[11] Competition in the field has led to both surgical innovation and price reduction over time, despite technological advances and increasing numbers of people seeking the procedure. Additionally, people who choose Lasik eye surgery are not hit with "surprise medical bills" since they know the costs up front and frequently pay out of pocket. This last point is important; unlike patients who are in need of urgent medical care—for, say, appendicitis or injuries sustained in a car accident—people *freely choose* to have Lasik eye surgery, and therefore have the freedom to compare prices and surgeons. In situations like this where patients are healthy enough to act as educated consumers with an array of options for nonurgent procedures, market forces can work in the way they are intended to.

The most obvious problem with applying free market principles to the delivery of health care is the fact that consuming health care, unlike having Lasik eye surgery, is rarely a free choice; all of us get sick at some point (some of us critically so), and all of us will die. Unlike the freedom of choice that comes with purchasing material commodities such as when we choose which car to buy, restaurant to dine in, or clothing store to shop in, the consumption of health care—after a debilitating stroke or traumatic injury, for instance—may come with no choice at all. A "consumer" may show up at the ED in kidney failure, as in the case of Mrs. McGaugh, unable to speak for herself. The ability to freely choose which ambulance to take, hospital to go to, and procedures to endure are, quite literally, impossible.

Unregulated free markets simply do not work in the context of health care, with the rare exception of elective procedures such as Lasik and cosmetic surgeries. In fact, economists acknowledge the limitations of unregulated free markets, even outside the context of health care. Robert Shiller, an economist at Yale University, argues that "standard economic theory is typically overenthusiastic about unregulated free markets. It usually ignores the fact that, given normal human weaknesses, an unregulated competitive economy will inevitably spawn an immense amount of manipulation and deception."[12]

Even if markets in health care are not intentionally manipulative and deceptive, they are, at best, amoral. Unregulated markets in health care cannot and do not question the ethical implications of making profit off the sick and vulnerable. Moreover, making money in our largely fee-for-service health care system *depends* on people being sick. There is, therefore, no incentive (with few exceptions) in this model to keep people well; hospitals need patients in beds, pharmaceutical companies need patients who need drugs, and insurers need their customers to see themselves as sick patients or future sick patients who are in need of medical care.

Precisely because so many of us in the United States are sicker than people in other comparable countries, profit abounds. The combined profits of thirteen major pharmaceutical companies from around the globe, for instance, was $744 billion during 2011–2018, and 45 percent of all these profits came from the United States alone.[13] While some may maintain that pharmaceutical companies require such hefty profits in order to make up their costs for research and development, when we take a closer look we can see that these profits far exceed the costs for research and development. Taken together, these thirteen companies spent only 17 percent of their revenue on research and development, while they spent nearly twice as much on advertising (27 percent of their revenue).[14] The health insurance industry has also continued to see tremendous growth, increasing its net earnings to $23.4 billion (a profit margin of 3.3 percent) in 2018 compared to net earnings of $16.1 (a profit margin of 2.4 percent) in 2017.[15] Most US hospitals also see huge revenue, collectively boasting higher profit margins than the pharmaceutical or insurance industries. While profits for individual hospitals vary (about one-quarter of both for-profit and not-for-profit hospitals lost money in 2016), according to one analysis in 2016 that looked across the United States' acute care hospitals, the total revenues exceeded expenses by more than $64 billion.[16]

While market logic might suggest that these profits are simply evidence of the market at work, the same logic would also suggest that market forces will lead to efficiency and decreased waste. This, however, is simply not the case in the US health care system. An Institute of Medicine report estimated that approximately 30 percent of health care spending in 2009 (about $750 billion) was "wasted on unnecessary services, excessive administrative costs, fraud, and other problems."[17] If this 30 percent ratio holds today—and there's no reason to think we've decreased this percentage—we're now above $1 trillion in waste.

This waste comes in many forms, including "defensive medicine," such as when doctors order expensive tests or procedures—even if they think they are unnecessary—out of fear of being sued for missing a rare finding. A 2010 study found that the annual medical liability system costs, which include defensive medicine, were around $55.6 billion in 2008.[18] Defensive medicine also leads to physicians and health care professionals spending more time documenting information in the EHR, bloating it with redundant information in an attempt to cover their bases in the event of future litigation. And this bloat is exponentially

The intersection of market logic with medicine's inherent tendency to fix, cure, and treat has led to a system that offers downstream, high-cost interventions for those who are able to afford them.

increased by the fact that the EHR is used primarily as a means of billing and coding visits and procedures, rather than as a way to document and plan for the care of patients. Ultimately, using the EHR as a way to bill for clinic visits, tests, and procedures leads to massive and redundant records as well as more time spent documenting patient encounters versus spending time with patients themselves. This is a significant problem given that more time spent working in the EHR can significantly contribute to clinician burnout. According to physicians Alexi Wright and Ingrid Katz,

> Increasing clerical burden is one of the biggest drivers of burnout in medicine. Time-motion studies show that for every hour physicians spend with patients, they spend one to two more hours finishing notes, documenting phone calls, ordering tests, reviewing results, responding to patient requests, prescribing medications, and communicating with staff. Little of this work is currently reimbursed. Instead, it is done in the interstices of life, during time often referred to as "work after work"—at night, on weekends, even on vacation.[19]

Whether caused by the EHR or not, burnout is particularly problematic not only because of the toll it takes on clinicians but also because doctors with symptoms of burnout are more likely to report having made a major medical error in the past three months and receive lower patient satisfaction scores.[20]

The extra work created by the EHR is simply one example of (and one of the many contributors to) the huge administrative burdens and costs of health care delivery. A 2020 study in the *Annals of Internal Medicine* found that administrative costs have increased to an astonishing 34 percent of the total health care expenditures in the United States, or nearly twice the percentage of Canada's administrative expenditures.[21] These costs, which are largely attributable to insurers' overhead associated with billing and reimbursement, are so significant that if the United States were to cut its administrative spending to that of Canadian levels, we could save more than $600 billion in a year's time. Speaking to *TIME* magazine, David Himmelstein, a professor at the City University of New York School of Public Health at Hunter College and coauthor of the study in the *Annals of Internal Medicine*, stated that "the difference [in administrative costs] between Canada and the U.S. is enough to not only cover all the uninsured but also to eliminate all the copayments and deductibles, and to amp up home care for the elderly and disabled . . . and frankly to have money left over."[22]

Such administrative costs and burdens are, in part, a result of a unique feature of the US health care system: the sheer amount of choice—choice of insurers, doctors, procedures, drugs, and interventions.[23] As a result, neither private nor public insurers have coordinated standards for setting prices, processing bills, and collecting payments, resulting in inefficiency and inconsistency. Some insurers, for example, require prior authorizations for procedures and prescriptions, and doctors' offices have responded to this by hiring full-time employees to negotiate with insurance companies, trying to secure prior authorizations and approvals that will allow physicians to provide the care they think is necessary for their patients. Insurance companies also employ people to approve or deny these requests, and such negotiations between insurers and doctors' offices can result in significant delays in care for patients.

The idealization of market principles like individual choice in the US health care system also manifests itself interpersonally during encounters between patients and clinicians. Internalizing principles that frame clinicians as "providers" and patients as "consumers" diminishes the need to engage in shared decision making in the clinical encounter. Rather than encouraging clinicians to draw on their experience and expertise to help guide patients with medical decisions, especially difficult ones about end-of-life care, market logic frames the clinical encounter as transactional in nature, circumscribing the clinician's role as a mere provider of options from which the patient can choose to consume.

The intersection of market logic with medicine's inherent tendency to fix, cure, and treat has led to a system where fee-for-service models are the norm, offering downstream, high-cost interventions for those who are able to afford them. As a result, US medicine emphasizes biological interventions after people get sick as opposed to preventive measures that might maintain health over a lifetime. This is why we hear health care professionals, politicians, and patients alike refer to our health care system as a "sick care" system. Because our pervasive fee-for-service model incentivizes fixing individual parts after they break rather than keeping patients well, specialty practices are thriving, pharmaceutical companies are booming, insurance companies reap huge annual profits, labs are bustling with work from redundant and often unnecessary workups, and private EHR companies generate unbelievable revenues while stifling attempts to create accessible patient information and coordinated care. Each of these independent markets grows fat off providing sick care solutions, all the while losing sight of the patient.

Also lost within this medical milieu are specialties that attempt to limit expensive procedures and focus instead on health promotion, such as primary care. In part because of its focus on avoiding unnecessary and frequently harmful medical interventions, primary care is among the least profitable medical specialties, with some primary care facilities struggling to stay afloat. As a result, primary care practices feel pressured to see as many patients as they can as quickly as possible. Indeed, research has shown that primary care physicians, in an effort to make clinic visits shorter and more efficient, may interrupt patients' opening statements within about twenty-three seconds, despite the fact that shorter visits can lead to unaddressed health issues and a superficial understanding of patient concerns.[24] While short visits may allow physicians to perform wellness screening exams for healthy people, or address routine medical problems like sore throats and earaches, they do not allow time for much else. Visits with patients who have multiple health concerns, or complicated issues like anxiety and depression, addiction, or chronic pain, require much more time than primary care visits currently allot if patients are to receive the care they deserve.

When patients don't have access to primary care or if their concerns are not fully addressed in abbreviated primary care visits, they may end up heading to the ED to receive care. According to UnitedHealth Group, such emergency room visits for conditions that are nonemergent costs the health care system about $32 billion a year. It also states that about two-thirds of ED visits by privately insured individuals are avoidable, meaning eighteen million visits to the ED each year could be effectively treated in the primary care setting, which is significant given that the average cost of treating nonemergent conditions in the ED is $2,032—twelve times higher than a doctor's office visit.[25] Nevertheless, for patients who are unable to have their health concerns adequately addressed during short primary care visits, or those who are uninsured and do not have access to a primary care clinician at all, a trip to the ED may feel like their best or only option.

Needless to say, the priorities of our medical system, which are guided by a commitment to generating revenues via procedures and tangible services, rarely emphasize caring well for patients—authentically listening to them, addressing their concerns, fears, and worries, and helping them make medical decisions that are aligned with their goals. This is precisely why providing quality primary palliative care is so difficult. A trusted primary care physician, someone who (ideally) might have developed a relationship over time with patients, and thus knows their values, preferences, and family dynamics, is the perfect person to have conversations about patients' priorities for end-of-life care, if and when the situation arises. Yet such conversations, which require time to listen, ask difficult questions, and respond to emotions, are anathema to a health care system focused on efficiency and productivity.

Even clinicians who have the heart and skills to engage in primary palliative care likely find themselves completely overwhelmed when they choose to do so. Physical progression toward the end of life often involves the slow failure of multiple organ systems, leading to the need for complex care. While patients nearing the end of life stand to benefit the most from the comprehensive, whole person care that a primary care physician can offer, time constraints and administrative demands like charting, billing, and collecting as well as synthesizing the recommendations of endless specialists can feel like a Herculean endeavor. As a result, most patients with serious or terminal illnesses inevitably receive fragmented, point-of-contact care from multiple specialists, emergency medicine doctors, and hospitalists with no one able to help them make sense of it all.

Real-Life Consequences

Recently, I cared for a thirty-eight-year-old mother in our ICU who was suffering from an unrelenting fungal infection in her lungs—a result of her uncontrolled diabetes. Because uncontrolled diabetes compromises a person's immune system, infections can more easily take hold and spread throughout the body, which happened with our patient. When I met with her nineteen-year-old daughter, Jamie, who was making medical decisions for her mother, she explained how her mom had been completely overwhelmed—emotionally, physically, and financially—since her dad had left the family two and a half years ago, leaving her mom alone with four children. Her mother had been working two jobs and also struggling with episodes of severe depression. Jamie said her mom seemed to grow increasingly tired, and she'd encouraged her to see a doctor months before she was hospitalized. Her mother, however, had neither the insurance coverage nor the financial means that would allow her to see a primary care clinician.

By the time her mother arrived at our ED, she was in diabetic ketoacidosis, meaning she didn't have enough insulin in her body to use sugar as fuel, so it started to break down fat instead, leading to a buildup of acids in the bloodstream called ketones. Left untreated, diabetic ketoacidosis can lead to loss of consciousness and even death. Though treatment in an ICU can help many patients with diabetic ketoacidosis, our patient was not getting any better due to the complications related to her severe infection. Despite our strongest antifungals, the infection continued to wreak havoc on her body.

Our team met with her daughter once more to talk about her mother's continual decline. I vividly remember when Jamie asked us why her mom wasn't improving and why any of this was happening at all. I recall it so well because I didn't know what to say. My gut reaction was to explain the infection again, but we'd had those conversations already, and I knew that was not what Jamie was asking. "I'm so sorry, Jamie," I said. "It's just not fair."

My response, it seemed, acknowledged what Jamie was thinking and feeling and gave her permission to grieve. As Jamie began to cry in our team's small conference room, I remember I wanted to cry too. The injustice of the situation felt overwhelming, given that her mother's initial condition was so easily treatable. A few visits in an outpatient clinic, some medications and lifestyle changes, and all this would have likely been avoided. Such care might have allowed her mother to go on living, as difficult as it was for her to navigate her new world as a single mother. Instead, her oldest child was now responsible for the family—and eventually for the decision of when to turn off her mother's ventilator and allow her to die.

Unbearably painful moments like these remind me that seeing health care as a commodity—something that should be dictated by the amoral forces of the free market—is at mortal odds with the good of patients. Ultimately, compassionate medicine focused on caring for patients well, even as they approach the end of life, disappears in the face of profit.

Market Forces and End-of-Life Care

Our health care system is designed in such a way that patients without insurance like Jamie's mom have no basic floor of care, except the ED when things get bad enough to warrant hospitalization. And strangely, if a patient like Jamie's mom is sick enough to get hospitalized, the system often responds by *over*treating since there is little incentive to not intervene, especially if patients have private insurance that will reimburse for such interventions. As T. R. Reid writes in *The Atlantic*,

> In other rich countries, there's a basic floor of care that everybody gets, which means there's a ceiling as well—the system simply won't pay for certain drugs or procedures. In the U.S., millions of people have no floor except the emergency room, and others have no ceiling. With the right insurance plan, there's almost no limit to what money can buy in American health care, regardless of the age or condition of the patient. And so we continue to spend huge sums on that small, generally elderly segment of the population with chronic illnesses, while millions have no health insurance.[26]

Patients with long-term chronic or terminal conditions can find themselves in a similar place at the end of life, even if they've had access to care throughout their illnesses. Our fragmented sick care system does little to coordinate the efforts of the various physicians caring for a single patient. Rather, patients' care is akin to an assembly line, where they are carried along, receiving care from a multitude of specialists at different points along the way. As mentioned previously, patients in their last six months of life may see ten or more individual specialists and experience multiple ED visits, hospital stays, and even ICU admissions in the last month of life.[27] At each point of care, specialists frequently concentrate only on their area of expertise and may lose sight of patients' overall trajectory and the bigger plan for care. Few of these specialists can see other clinicians' notes buried within inaccessible EHR systems, let alone intentionally coordinate their efforts with one another in the care of their shared patients. Consequently, each point of care comes with new information, new options and fixes, and more costs. Patients are presented with a menu of options at each point, and may have no one to help them discern which options make the most sense in the context of their goals and values.

Because difficult conversations about patients' wishes for their end-of-life care rarely happen in such a fragmented system, many patients end up continually seeking and receiving care until they reach the end of the line. For many, the end of the line looks like receiving treatment just days before death, a trip to the ED in an ambulance like Mrs. McGaugh, or dying in the hospital instead of at home like Nicole's mom. And it's easy for those looking at such situations from the outside, even clinicians, to ask themselves why patients would "irrationally" choose such an end, without recognizing that many are simply following the path set before them. In a system that makes it so much easier to present patients with an endless array of options than to engage in difficult conversations about inevitable death, choosing to jump off the assembly line earlier doesn't seem like much of an option at all.

Too often, a hospice or palliative team is called in at the end of this line, when other options have evaporated or medical teams have decided that patients and their families are "in denial" and preoccupied with ideas of "futile" care—despite the fact that patients' and families' decisions are typically in line with the previous decisions that led up to them. Nevertheless, when hospice or palliative care is initiated near the end, it appears as nothing more than a soft landing for patients who desperately, fearfully, or even reluctantly decide to jump off the assembly line at the last possible moment. And such last-minute decisions—which are all too common—simply perpetuate ideas about hospice and palliative care being equivalent to "giving up."

Hospice care and palliative medicine were not intended to be options of last resort. Rather, they developed as a humanistic response to a health care system that failed to adequately attend to the suffering of patients with serious illnesses. In Saunders's words, hospice care intends to help patients know that "they matter" until the end of their lives and that hospice will not only help people die peacefully but also help them "live until [they] die."[28] This philosophy of care, which centers on the quality of a person's life, runs counter to the larger health care system's orientation toward biological intervention and fee-for-service care. Because of the emphasis on quality of life over more interventions, it may not be surprising that even during the most difficult and complex phase of life, this new philosophy of care did much more than improve the lived experience of patients with advanced illness; it did so while also reducing the costs associated with end-of-life care.[29]

For better or worse, hospice and palliative medicine's ability to save money has played a major role in the development of the field of end-of-life care. It would be naive to believe that hospice care's rapid expansion in the 1970s and 1980s (not to mention its inclusion as a Medicare benefit in 1982) as well as the recent, rapid expansion of palliative medicine are not largely attributable to this fact alone. Indeed, palliative medicine programs are becoming increasingly more common within hospital settings where they have proven to curtail end-of-life expenses, thereby potentially improving hospitals' profit margins.[30] Many see such cost savings as critical given the tendency to point, inaccurately, to the extraordinary spending associated with care for patients at the end of life. While it is true that only 5 percent of patients account for 50 percent of health care dollars, it is not the case that all these patients are at the end of life. In fact, in 2011, researchers Melissa Aldridge and Amy Kelley found that among patients with the highest health care costs, only 11 percent were in their last year of life. Of the $1.6 trillion spent on personal health care costs in the United States that year, 13 percent was dedicated to the care of patients at the end of life.[31] While there is no doubt that this is a significant amount of money, these figures suggest that end-of-life care is not the major culprit for the runaway cost of health care in the United States—a cost undoubtedly driven up by the expensive, fragmented, hyper-specialized care that defines US medicine.

Despite the fact that less money is spent on patients at the end of life than many people think—which means that the amount of cost savings attributed to hospice and palliative care may be overstated—this has not tempered the health care system's zeal to adopt hospice care and palliative medicine as tools to save money.[32] Unlike the vast majority of other medical specialties that are entrenched in fee-for-service models, much of the work within both hospice care and palliative medicine must be proven via the language of cost savings. For instance, because more savings are seen in the context of hospital medicine when patients choose to stop aggressive (and expensive) treatments and transition to comfort care only, those of us in palliative medicine have a harder time garnering financial support for efforts to offer palliative medicine in outpatient settings where we can provide care earlier in the illness trajectory and keep patients feeling better and for longer. When the real benefit (that is, real cost savings) of palliative medicine is perceived to be in the hospital setting, there is little incentive to invest in outpatient clinics, even when doing so is in the best interests of patients with chronic and life-limiting illnesses.

Rather than seeing hospice and palliative medicine as care dedicated to the lived experience of illness (the kind of care that all medicine should be offering every patient), the US health care system sees them as a means to limit costly care for incurable patients. In this way, the health care system has eagerly taken hospice care and palliative medicine into its mighty grasp, medicalizing and monetizing their efforts.

The Value of Concurrent Care

When hospice care and palliative medicine are consigned to being the place where patients go when there is "nothing else for them," their ability to care for patients earlier in their illness journey and potential to influence the broader culture of medicine are both significantly undermined. Add to this the suggestion that this care is important *because of its ability to save money*, and it's no wonder that hospice and palliative medicine have remained so limited in scope.

Consider the limited role of hospice care, for instance. Aside from rare exceptions, a patient may enroll in hospice *or* continue active treatment, but a patient cannot pursue both—in part because hospice saves the health care system money when expensive, disease-directed therapies are stopped. When the Medicare Hospice Benefit was enacted in 1982, it did and still does require that patients accept "the palliative rather than curative nature of hospice care" in order to ensure that the costs of hospice care would be offset by reduced expenditures for aggressive treatment.[33] Many have argued that such provisions force patients to make "a terrible choice" between treatment and hospice services, which becomes a barrier to hospice utilization.[34] For many patients, this decision to stop active treatment can feel too extreme, even if they are ready to start considering other options. Thus the need to make such extreme, all-or-nothing decisions perpetuates delayed decisions to transition to hospice, even when patients stand to benefit immensely from their services.

Moreover, forcing an all-or-nothing decision in order to enroll in hospice does not help to identify patients who are sicker or nearer to the end of their lives. Studies have shown that patients who choose to forgo life-sustaining treatment and enroll in hospice are not necessarily those who are in greater need of hospice's services, or even think they are in greater need.[35] In fact, many patients who do not choose to enroll in hospice and forgo active treatment would benefit as much as—if not more than—those patients who do choose to forgo. Studies examining the use of hospice within the US Department of Veterans Affairs (VA) suggest as much. In 2009, the VA launched the Comprehensive End-of-Life Care Initiative to improve quality end-of-life care by offering hospice care concurrently with active treatment in order to increase the use of hospice services. Subsequent research on this effort has shown that increasing the availability of hospice care without restricting disease-directed treatments for veterans with advanced lung cancer was associated with less aggressive interventions and significantly lower costs, while still providing cancer treatment.[36]

The cost savings associated with concurrent care seems to defy logic. But these savings highlight the remarkable value of patient-centered care: when patients are given the safety, support, and coordination that hospice care provides—along with the opportunities to have discussions about their values and preferences—earlier in their journey, they actually choose for themselves to forgo invasive treatments as death approaches. Patients, for instance, who participate in Aetna's Compassionate Care Program—which allows patients to enroll in hospice while continuing disease-focused treatment and offers them specialized nurse case management—are less likely to have inpatient hospital stays and more likely to fully enter hospice sooner than those who do not participate in the program.[37] Programs like this one that allow for concurrent care lead to better patient outcomes while also reducing unnecessary admissions and the associated costs in the last ninety days of life. It seems that when we allow patients to receive hospice care without forcing them to forgo active treatment, most patients are able to intuit when the burdens of treatment begin to outweigh the benefits and then feel more comfortable easing into comfort care only when that time comes.

Offering patients the kind of care that hospice and palliative medicine provides, regardless of whether patients are ready to "give up" on curative treatment, is not only the right thing to do but also the most sensible thing to do. The good news is that in addition to these initiatives by Aetna and the VA, the Affordable Care Act made some important steps toward eliminating—or at least questioning the utility of—the strict trade-off between curative and hospice services by authorizing a demonstration project to assess the effect of concurrent care on quality of life, patient care, and cost effectiveness.[38] The Centers for Medicare and Medicaid Services invited 141 hospices to participate in the five-year project, which began in January 2016 and is currently still running. It is the first Medicare hospice demonstration project in thirty-five years.

Our hope is that this demonstration project, along with the research coming out of programs like the VA's, will encourage earlier initiation of hospice services not contingent on patients making all-or-nothing decisions. We know, however, that in our market-driven health care system, the decision to allow concurrent care across the board will largely come down to dollars and cents. And we also know that even if concurrent care does prove to be cost effective and health systems do start to encourage concurrent care, this alone is not enough to shift the culture of medicine—a culture that at its core, struggles to confront the realities of suffering and death. As physician and professor of public health Ashish K. Jha puts it,

> Ultimately, our failings in adequately caring
> for patients at the end of life come from the
> difficulties we have, both as patients and physicians,
> in confronting mortality. This is not a health care
> financing problem, but a fundamentally human
> problem. Physicians and nurses are often hesitant
> to have discussions with patients about their care
> preferences near the end of life. Care at the end of
> life is every bit as important as policy makers have
> thought, just not for the reasons often cited. . . .
> It's essential to avoid getting distracted by promises
> of cost savings along the way.[39]

Where to from Here?

It should be said that market logic is so pervasive in medicine that even clinicians in end-of-life care are not impervious to its pressure. While hospice care does not function within a fee-for-service model—and therefore is much less profitable compared to other medical specialties—new, for-profit hospice agencies are increasing in number. The vast majority of these for-profit agencies are high-quality, patient-oriented organizations. Yet as with any market-based system, regulation is necessary in order to prevent self-interested decisions, such as cherry-picking patients who are less sick (and thus less expensive to care for), providing subpar services, or engaging in other manipulative practices in order to offer less care to patients as a means of retaining more of the per diem payment that comes from Medicare. Prioritizing profits in the care of the sick is problematic in all areas of medicine, but it is particularly unconscionable in end-of-life care.

Suffice it to say, the pervasive free market principles that guide our health care system do not and cannot incentivize the kind of human care that is impossible to measure in dollars and cents. In fact, these principles encourage more treatment and procedures along with less coordination of care, all of which can be harmful to patients, especially those who are chronically or terminally ill. We know that invasive procedures at the end of life are causing more suffering and the conversations that could prevent these invasive procedures are not happening often or early enough.[40] So how do we encourage clinicians to take time to slow down and discern their patients' values and goals so that they can better respond to the lived experiences of illness and suffering, even when the health care system disincentivizes such approaches to patient care?

We alluded earlier to the need for clinicians, regardless of their medical specialty, to practice primary palliative care. Unlike traditional hospice care, palliative care can be offered concurrently with curative treatments, and the principles of palliative care should inform the approach all clinicians take when caring for patients with serious illnesses. However, given the constraints of our system that lead to short visits and abbreviated clinical encounters, and given the fact that specialists run busy practices managing complex information, offering robust palliative care in addition to their everyday work can feel impossible. Nevertheless, we believe that even when addressing all their patients' palliative needs is unrealistic, all clinicians can offer their specialized care in a way that is deeply informed by patients' values and goals.

In *Being Mortal*, Gawande shares an example of this approach, describing the kind of care he provided for a patient with cancer that had advanced to the point that it was obstructing her bowels, ultimately requiring surgery. Gawande recounts how he initially offered his patient a "menu of options" and "reverted to being Dr. Informative—here are the facts and figures; what do you want us to do?" before he stepped back, slowed down, and

The free market
principles that guide our
health care system do
not incentivize the kind
of human care that is
impossible to measure
in dollars and cents.

took the time to discuss his patient's goals, hopes, fears, and values.[41] This conversation allowed him to work together with his patient to tailor a care plan that included surgery to relieve symptoms of the obstruction, as long as Gawande did not take any "risky chances" during the operation that might lead to more suffering, which is what his patient feared the most. The choices Gawande finally made during the operation—which were informed by his patients' wishes—avoided excessive risk. Although the operation did not fully resolve the obstruction, it did lead to improved symptoms, allowing the patient to spend more quality time with her family before she died, which is what she wanted most.

We believe that all clinicians should practice medicine in a similar way and allow the principles of palliative medicine, which focus on meaning, values, and quality of life, to inform the care they offer to all patients. Patients *want to know* how treatments, procedures, or medications may affect their lives, or whether these interventions will promote or diminish their goals for care, especially if their time is limited. In the United States, we have legions of primary care physicians who are up to this task; virtually all of them have been trained to treat patients as whole people, understand the need to identify their patients' values, and want to engage in conversations about goals of care. And yet, within our current health care system, these same clinicians feel pressured to maintain high throughput and engage in short, truncated visits focused on just one or two problems. While some clinicians still find ways to have meaningful end-of-life discussions despite these constraints, changing how we define, incentivize, assess, and reward "quality care" has the potential to revolutionize how practitioners from across medical specialties spend time with their patients.

We know that all clinicians can do a better job communicating with patients about their goals and values, but we also recognize that some clinicians might feel uncomfortable, ill prepared, or poorly equipped to have conversations that move beyond these details and begin to tread into the territory of end-of-life decisions. And that's OK; it's OK for clinicians to refer patients to a palliative medicine team if they feel uncomfortable having conversations themselves about death and dying. At a minimum, all clinicians, regardless of specialty, should be able to *recognize* when patients are suffering in ways that extend beyond their bodies, and when conversations about goals and values or transitions to hospice care are warranted. And if they feel uncomfortable navigating these admittedly difficult conversations themselves, they should consult a palliative medicine clinician and encourage their patients to earnestly seek out what palliative medicine has to offer. Connecting patients to such care should not be seen as the last resort for when there is nothing left to offer but rather as an opportunity for patients to reflect on what's most important to them and receive coordinated care that honors those important things, helping them live with less pain, anxiety, and discomfort as well as potentially more joy, hope, and freedom.

Palliative medicine is not about last resorts. And it's not about saving money. It's about giving people the opportunity to live out the rest of their lives, however long that might be, with purpose and intention. It's about giving people a bit more control over how they want to live and die.

It's about caring for people the way so many of us in medicine always imagined we would.

FACING DEATH TOGETHER

While I gained vast technological knowledge during my training, my spirit—the compassion and humanity I had brought with me to medical school . . . began to atrophy. . . . I went into medical school a human being, and I came out a doctor.

—Jessica Nutik Zitter

Facing death is hard. And it's hard for all of us. As Irvin Yalom remarks, "It's like trying to stare the sun in the face: you can only stand so much of it."[1] As a result, we've devised all sorts of things to shroud death's painful glare—religious narratives, biological and evolutionary explanations, myths, fables, and medical interventions. Even our medical interventions aimed at making death less painful and frightening can serve to conceal death's terror.

The need for and benefits of hospice and palliative care cannot be overstated. And quality end-of-life conversations that address a person's hopes and wishes for the rest of their time on this earth are critical for caring well for the people who need it most. And yet these conversations are not happening nearly enough, and as a result too few people get the chance to experience the benefits of hospice and palliative care. When Shawn tells me about the times he talks to patients and families about their hopes and fears about dying, he says he often gets questions from his patients about why they didn't get to see him sooner or why no one else had talked to them before. When he tells me these things, it reminds me of my own experience, how those conversations didn't happen with my mom and our family until it was too late, how we were always waiting for the "right moment" with my dad, and how that right moment never came. It reminds me that we still live and die in a medical system that struggles to address the ways we suffer beyond our bodies. Despite the progress that has been made in end-of-life care, most medical professionals and patients are still too afraid to stare death in the face.

Elsewhere I have written extensively about our shared existential anxiety in the face of death and how that anxiety plays out in medicine in particular.[2] While it is true that all of us are tempted to turn away from the anxiety that our mortality produces, medicine offers a pretty convenient means for health care professionals to do so: in focusing on the biological happenings of the body—talking about lab results, individual organ systems, or treatments left to try—health care professionals don't have to acknowledge human frailty and vulnerability. In short, the way medicine is practiced and clinicians are trained both offer health care professionals an all-too-easy means of turning away from suffering and mortality. When they see themselves as people who are trained to fix or cure patients by intervening in biological processes, there is no perceived need to attend to suffering beyond the physical body. Consequently, medical practice and culture have in a lot of ways become masters at evading questions about suffering and death.

Of course this is not always the case; there are clinicians who grapple with these questions all the time, and they are probably better clinicians for it. But for the most part, avoiding these questions and focusing on the biological body that can be assessed and treated is much more comfortable than grappling with existential questions about suffering and human finitude. And when patients receive care in a system like this, they may develop unrealistic expectations for what medicine can do for them, thinking there is always "something to do." Framing medicine as an endeavor focused only on (temporary) biological fixes is unfair for everyone involved; it limits the kind of care clinicians offer and patients expect to receive.

What I have learned from my experiences with my own parents along with my time with medical students, residents, and clinical colleagues is that medicine is so much more than caring for the biological body. Medicine is painful and beautiful. It's overflowing with meaning, vulnerability, and opportunities for human connection. I've learned that health professionals have one of the most incredible jobs on the planet. They have opportunities to care for people who need it most, and in doing so, see people at their best and worst. They have opportunities to learn that life is fragile and finite, relationships are all that matter, that there is so much suffering in the world and also so much joy.

Despite all this meaning, however, medical professionals rarely talk about any of it. And students are certainly not prepared to deal with all this humanness. We don't tell them that a life in health care has just as much to do with their hearts as it does their minds. In fact, we often sell them a bill of goods as undergrads that is nothing like the real world of health care. We frame medicine as an "applied science." We tell them that if they're good at chemistry and biology, or like the human body, they'll be good clinicians. And then as soon as they start seeing patients, they learn quickly that no one told them it would be like this—that they would see so much pain and suffering and patients would have unanswerable questions about why they got sick and can't be fixed. We don't tell them that they will take care of babies who die and older patients who suffer alone and that they will see so much poverty and addiction and mental anguish. We don't explain that they will have moments of success and triumph and moments of exhaustion and regret.

Professor Kathryn Montgomery points out in her book *How Doctors Think* that medicine frames itself as an applied science, even though clinicians have the good sense not to practice it that way.[3] Clinicians know about uncertainty and the need for gut feelings or clinical intuition; they know that patients' experiences can be unpredictable and things can go wrong, even when they least expect it. They know that medicine is a *practice*, uncertain through and through. This is not to say that things like objectivity, accuracy, and scientific evidence are unimportant; they're absolutely critical. Evidence-based medicine, objective measurements, and precise tests are necessary and good. Such things save lives and give us important answers to pressing questions. But when it comes to the lived, human experience of medicine, they can only offer us partial answers. We can't pretend that technical knowledge translates into an ability to recognize and attend to patients' existential suffering. Part of what makes medicine so difficult—and so incredible—is that it asks the hardest questions, all those deep, abiding, unavoidable questions that don't have satisfactory answers. Whether we like it or not, medicine is a concentration of all the elements of the human condition right in front of our eyes.

Nevertheless, we have failed to tell students about any of this. Not only that, but we recruit them into an educational system that subtly works against vulnerability, de-emphasizing human connection. What many people don't realize, especially those who get frustrated with their doctors and other caregivers, is that in so many ways, it is not their clinician's fault. We have trained them in a system that conflates professionalism with productivity and compassion with objectivity. The culture in which clinicians practice and trainees learn is shaped by medicine's epistemology—that is, what doctors know and how they come to know it. Medicine is seen as an applied science, so the "knowable" is believed to be observable and measurable facts, and how one comes to know those facts is through observation, measurements, lab tests, imaging, and the like.

The problem is, epistemology shapes ideas about the kinds of qualities that will allow students or medical professionals to properly secure the knowledge they "need." So things like objectivity, rigor, and clinical detachment are seen as virtues; embodying them is seen as the proper and professional way to be.[4] As a result, students may come to see the adoption of an objective stance toward patients and their illness as good, noble, or right—despite the fact that scientific objectivity can obscure the very human elements of illness and medicine.

When medical professionals' roles are framed in such a way that objective distance and productivity are seen as virtues, it denies the human connection that is possible between patients and their caregivers. And this connection is crucial. As medical humanist Ronald Carson puts it, "I want my doctor to tell me the medical meanings of my symptoms, to be sure, but I also want some help in grasping the personal significance of my malady. I want both to have my 'otherness' acknowledged and to be recognized as still belonging to the tribe of the living."[5]

Students and their clinical mentors have few, if any, opportunities to express how the practice of medicine affects them, how encounters with suffering, death, and meaninglessness take an emotional toll, and why distancing themselves from the realities of suffering and death seems like their best and only option. Medical education and practice don't allow them to connect to the most meaningful parts of their work or see their patients as teachers who can show them what it looks like to live or die well. We know that medicine is more than science, but we still emphasize the scientific and technical aspects above all else. And when we do that, it is only natural to make claims about the need to stay objective or maintain clinical distance when taking care of patients.

I've too often seen the consequences of this kind of education. Students tell me how painful it is to experience their first code and then have no one to talk to about it. Or worse, they hear medical staff making dismissive remarks or jokes while it's happening. I've had residents tell me that they regret ever having gone into medicine, and physicians tell me that they feel completely disconnected from meaning and purpose, from the reasons they went into medicine in the first place. A few months ago, I had a resident in my office who said that there was "something wrong with him." He said that a baby he delivered had died in a way that was particularly traumatic for everyone in the room. He said his attending seemed fine, so he should be fine too. "There's something wrong with me," he told me. "I shouldn't be so upset about this."

It's moments like these that help me understand why health care and health care education tend to avoid vulnerability, or why a health care professional would focus so much on the biological body. In the face of tragedy, it's much easier to think about how to manage the physical care of a patient than confront the realities of human frailty and finitude. It's especially tempting to do this when no one has prepared new professionals for the realities of taking care of people who are sick or scared or dying. And nowhere is this lack of preparation more obvious and problematic than in end-of-life care. As Diane Meier, director of the Center to Advance Palliative Care, explains,

Patients and families . . . assume that doctors will tell them when time is running out, what to expect, and how best to navigate these unknown and frightening waters. But many doctors don't do these things. Most are, in fact, completely untrained in these aspects of the human experience. Medical school and residency have traditionally provided little or no training on how to continue to care for patients when disease-modifying treatments no longer work. . . . [P]hysicians do what we have been trained to do: order more tests, more procedures, more treatments, even when these things no longer help. Even when they no longer make sense.[6]

As a medical educator myself, I can attest to the fact that we have a long way to go when it comes to preparing future doctors for critical conversations and navigating care for patients at the end of life. Part of the reason for this is that the Liaison Committee on Medical Education (LCME), the organization that accredits medical schools in the United States and ensures they are meeting national standards, does not have any standards related to providing education about palliative care, nor does it require rotations or courses in palliative medicine. While it does state that schools should teach students elements of "end-of-life care," not mentioning that students need palliative care education specifically leaves a gap in medical school curricula as well as perpetuates the misconception that palliative and end-of-life care are synonymous.[7]

Physician Barbara Head and her colleagues argue that until the LCME mandates that medical schools include education about palliative care, schools may avoid doing so given their already-crowded curricula.[8] Because the content that needs to be covered in medical school is so vast, and because information about palliative medicine and end-of-life care is significantly underrepresented in medical licensing exams, these topics often get short shrift in medical training. Indeed, during the course of their research for their book on care for the dying, Christine and Robert Cowgill contacted 122 medical schools and 34 nursing schools regarding coursework and training in the areas of palliative, emotional, and spiritual care to the dying and found that only 8 of these medical schools and none of these nursing schools had mandatory coursework in those areas of study, and only 16 offered elective coursework.[9]

Though disappointing, these findings are not surprising. Medical education was conspicuously late to the game when it came to teaching students about death and dying. An article from the mid-1970s, for instance, found that between 1960 and 1971, not one article existed in the medical education literature on teaching medical students about death and dying.[10] It wasn't until 1972 that the first description of a course on death and dying—an elective course offered at Vanderbilt University—appeared in the literature. Fortunately, by the 1980s, the number of similar courses increased at medical schools across the country, with more than half of schools offering some kind of education on death and dying, elective or otherwise.[11]

Yet still today the issue remains that while education on death and dying might exist, it appears too infrequently or sporadically in medical curricula. As a result, some students see education on death and dying as extraneous to their "real" medical education. Like Head and her colleagues point out, it is not uncommon for both students and faculty to view palliative care curriculum as "optional."[12] Because of this—and because palliative care content is woefully underrepresented or totally absent on standardized exams—students come to see palliative care knowledge and skills as not foundational to their medical education or future practice.

The dearth of palliative care education is not unique to medical education in the United States, however. Surveys of medical students across the globe suggest that students value palliative medicine and *want* more opportunities to develop the knowledge and skills needed for caring for patients who are chronically ill and dying, but students continue to feel ill prepared for such care when they graduate. This is a result of the fact that educational efforts in palliative care in both the United States and abroad are often transient, not practical or experiential (many schools simply offer online training modules), and lack necessary institutional and financial support, with much of the foundational work being created with limited grant funding.[13]

Some might hope that if medical students have not had opportunities to develop their capacity to address suffering and provide end-of-life care by the time they graduate, they might get these chances during their residency training. This is not the case, though. Despite the fact that residents find themselves engaging in critical, end-of-life conversations with patients much more frequently than they did as medical students, many of them receive little to no training during their residencies. One recent study found that 88 percent of residents reported little to no classroom training on end-of-life care in their residency programs, even though half the residents reported they'd engaged in more than ten end-of-life conversations with patients.[14] Residents also stated that they often have these conversations with patients on their own, with 60 percent of residents saying that these conversations were not supervised by their attending physicians.

Similarly, a study out of the United Kingdom found that residents' feelings of inadequacy around end-of-life care are a result of both insufficient training in medical school and poor instruction from their mentors in residency training. One participant in the study, for instance, observed, "I think at medical school we learn a lot about trying to get people better, but not so much about what to do when they don't." Another said, "To be honest . . . I think we get distracted by so many other things, like just memorizing disease and pathologies and treatments, that I think I overlooked [care for the dying]." While reflecting on their first year of residency training, the young doctors in the study indicated that the majority of their clinical mentors did not engage in end-of-life care and spent little time teaching it to new residents. Moreover, all the participants described death as being "taboo" within the hospital culture, and some suggested that older physician mentors "continued to focus on cure" and wanted to keep treating, despite perceived futility. As one participant noted, "I guess it's the whole concept that if someone dies it's a failure. And that's still there; it just permeates the whole thing." When talking about his older mentors, another participant stated that "they come around and say: 'Right, can't do anything about this, going to die, palliative care.' . . . [W]e just sort of called palliative care and it was their job."[15]

Research like this is disappointing to say the least, especially because real-life experiences with clinical mentors caring for patients who are suffering or dying can have such a profound effect on trainees. Leaders in palliative medicine argue that learning to care for these patients who are suffering or at the end of life cannot be taught in lectures or through demonstrations. Rather, such things are learned through experiences with patients and guidance from quality clinical mentors. As physician Susan Block at Harvard Medical School says, "The only way to improve competencies [in end-of-life care] is through field practice and feedback." Encouraging trainees to authentically engage with patients and hear their stories, learn what their lived experiences are like, and reflect on what it might mean to be in their situation can be transformative for students. Fortunately, there are a few medical schools in the United States that have recently taken the initiative to provide these kinds of real-life experiences for students. Tufts University School of Medicine, Larner College of Medicine at the University of Vermont, the University of California, San Francisco School of Medicine, Perelman School of Medicine at the University of Pennsylvania, and others are beginning to uniquely and longitudinally incorporate palliative care training into their curricula.[16]

These changes are promising—and they're critical given that experiences with patients who are suffering or dying can teach students about compassion, care, and mortality in a way that they won't learn anywhere else. When Head and her colleagues evaluated a new, required palliative care course for third-year medical students at the University of Louisville, their findings suggested as much. In addition to learning about quality medical treatment for the dying, students stated in written reflections that their time on the rotation helped them understand the lived experience of patients and families, showed them what it means to be a doctor, and taught them about themselves—their strengths and limitations, ways to become a better physician, and how to begin to personally cope with death. Looking back on the course, one student stated that "it's easy to wander in and out of patient's rooms without really ever stopping to think about how I am wandering in and out of another human being's life. When I stop to think about it, I feel completely undeserving." Another student commented that they "came to understand Mr. Smith more. To me, he became a person and no longer a patient to try and fix," while another said that the experience "made me remember why I had initially wanted to pursue medicine."[17]

Given these outcomes, it's unfortunate that students enrolled in the majority of medical schools across the country have to intentionally seek out similar opportunities—opportunities that are foundational to their personal and professional development. I have seen firsthand how transformative experiences with patients at the end of life can be for students, both those whom I work with and those I've known in my personal life.

No matter who we are—medical students or not—personal experiences with another's suffering can change the way we see the world and ourselves in that world. But for those going into medicine, such experiences should be requisite. All trainees, regardless of the specialty they pursue, will encounter patients who are suffering or dying, and they need to know how to care for these patients. To put it bluntly, not preparing future health care professionals to care for patients approaching the end of life (or preparing them to *at least* know when they need to consult a specialist to help them with such care) is irresponsible and potentially harmful for patients.

Research indicates that students *want* to learn more about end-of-life care outside the typical "breaking bad news" lectures as well as ways to cope with emotions surrounding death and dying, because students believe that experiences with death can "allow them to grow as individuals and doctors."[18] Therefore, encouraging students to spend time with dying patients in a way that allows these patients to teach others what their dying *means* to them, and how they have (or have not) made sense of their suffering, offers students the unique opportunity to see and respond to the more subjective, experiential, and non-medicalized side of patient care.

Looking Forward: Making End-of-Life Care Part of Everyday Care

What I have learned over the years is that medicine is full of people who care about others and went into medicine because they want to make a difference. Unfortunately, much of their education and training poorly equips them to do so when it comes to patients who suffer in ways that extend beyond their physical bodies or who need guidance at the end of life. Medical education encourages stoicism more often than humility and values technical skill and scientific acumen over compassion and communication. Medical training does not encourage future doctors to talk about the fact that patients' experiences—which can be frightening and tragic—are stark reminders of their own potential for sickness and death. And given that medicine frames itself as an applied science, it feels almost natural for people to make claims about the need for objectivity and clinical distance, and thus turn away from all this vulnerability and pretend it doesn't exist. What I try to remind my own medical students is that both knowledge and emotions matter, that the best diagnosticians are the ones who know the medical literature and evidence-based medicine practices—but who also trust their gut feelings—and listen well to patients' stories in order to paint the whole picture. I remind them that medicine is not an art or science but instead a strange amalgamation of the two that can't be separated at all, that being a good physician means you know *and* feel things, that they can't pretend they aren't sometimes affected by what they see. They can't pretend vulnerability isn't part of the job.

The question that remains, however, is how we help future health care professionals see that helping patients navigate big decisions at the end of life, and knowing when to take a pause to talk to patients about these things, is just as important as diagnosing and treating diseases. One way to do this is to help students give up the "science claim," as Montgomery says, and recognize that medicine, nursing, and occupational and physical therapy (the list goes on) are all caring professions where people are called to care for whole people, not just their biological bodies.[19] This involves a commitment to thinking about *who students are becoming* on their journey toward a career in health care as well as an effort to create an educational environment that holds a space for vulnerability—an environment that encourages students to reflect on their experiences with patients and on those difficult questions that everyone has but no one asks out loud.

There are medical and health professions schools across the country, including my own, that are taking personal formation and character development seriously and are incorporating opportunities for reflection and connection to patients. But I sometimes wonder if these efforts are enough when it comes to learning to care for patients at the end of life. Students learn quickly that ideals like compassion and empathy only go so far when you're being trained by busy residents and attendings who work in a system so focused on productivity. In the morass of contemporary US medicine, where the commercial interests of a broken health care system intersect with conflicting calls for both compassion and detachment, clinicians and students are left at a confusing crossroads when it comes to taking time to understand what is most important to patients. The goals of training and practice get distorted in such an environment, and the potential for real connection with patients gets drowned out by the perceived need for efficiency and productivity.

It's undeniable that our health care system, which largely relies on fee-for-service delivery models, does little to encourage physicians to engage in conversations that are time consuming and emotionally difficult (though often emotionally rewarding). Yet it's too simplistic to say that the only reason doctors avoid difficult conversations is because of a lack of financial incentives or due to time constraints. It is true that the fast-paced work of doctors makes it difficult to find the time needed to discuss difficult issues, but we can't forget that under the Affordable Care Act, physicians are now reimbursed through Medicare for conversations with patients about advance care planning.[20] This is a huge step in the right direction given that physicians were previously unable to bill for the time they spent with patients discussing options for end-of-life care. Nevertheless, these financial incentives are not enough to change the culture surrounding death and dying in medicine. As Meier points out, "Policies aimed at fundamental change in physicians' behavior will require more than financial incentives." She goes on to say,

Doctors care deeply about their patients. . . . To change behavior, we must change the education and training of young physicians and the professional and clinical culture in which they practice. New doctors should learn about the management of symptoms [and] how to relay bad news, how to stand with patients and their families until death, and how to help patients and families make the best use of their remaining time together.[21]

Are All Doctors Called to Provide This Care?

When we look at the kind of hyperspecialized care that medicine now offers, it is tempting to say that there are some medical specialties where physicians don't need to "stand with patients and their families until death," or medical specialties where patients should hope for an expert technician rather than a compassionate person. I have many times heard people say, especially when they are referring to a specialized surgical procedure, that it doesn't matter how friendly or compassionate their doctor is, as long as the doctor is skilled and competent. While I understand the sentiment behind this—competence does, indeed, matter—I can't seem to understand why so many frame it this way, as if it is a zero-sum game, as if one quality somehow can't exist alongside the other. There are so many physicians and surgeons who embody both these qualities. One obvious example is Gawande, a successful surgeon who also finds connecting with patients and caring for them as they age and decline so important that he wrote a best-selling book about it. Another is Kalanithi, a neurosurgery resident whose training was defined by masterful precision and yet who still understood that technical skill was not enough for a life in medicine. In his astounding memoir *When Breath Becomes Air*, written while he was dying of cancer in his late thirties, Kalanithi says, "The physician's duty is not to stave off death or return patients to their old lives, but to take into our arms a patient and family whose lives have disintegrated and work until they can stand back up and face, and make sense of, their own existence."[22]

These, of course, are famous examples and might be seen as exceptional; some may believe Gawande and Kalanithi are outliers or atypical physicians who embody both great technical skill and deep compassion. Yet Shawn and I work every day with physicians, nurses, and other health care professionals who are technically gifted and also unspeakably empathic—people who care whether patients live and die in ways that align with their values. While we wish we knew more health care professionals like this, we know enough of them to say that it's completely reasonable to expect that the person taking care of you possesses both the medical expertise to care for your body and sensitivity to care about your being.

It's completely reasonable to expect that the person taking care of you possesses both the medical expertise to care for your body and sensitivity to care about your being.

This is not to say that all health care professionals have the capacity or the will to grapple with deep existential questions about human mortality and suffering. Many involved in patient care would rather not dwell on death and sickness, or the fragility of the human mind and body, and with good reason: it's hard to stay upbeat in a world filled with such grim realities. Still, all health care professionals should be able to acknowledge the vulnerability inherent in caring for those who are sick and suffering. They must acknowledge that virtually all patients suffer and all people die, and sometimes more medical care is not always what's needed.

Health care professionals, and especially physicians, should be trained to recognize when more medical care actually harms patients and how to stop the wheels of medicine from turning—and hopefully stop them a little sooner on the path. Too often we see physicians who wait until their patients' situations are too dire to even consider switching gears. Whether this is a result of pride or ego, a desire to continue with treatment because they care too much for patients to "let them go," or because they feel poorly equipped to navigate conversations about transitioning to end-of-life care, the fact is that too many patients and families confront the end of life abruptly, unexpectedly, and far too late in their journey. So even if physicians feel like they cannot initiate the conversation themselves, they should recognize when patients are stuck on a path that might lead to more suffering and then consult the team of health care professionals who can begin the conversations that some physicians might not feel equipped to have themselves. At the very least, patients should be able to trust that they are being cared for in a medical system that is working in their best interest and that someone will take the time to talk to them and discern their wishes so that they'll receive care that is shaped by their values. When it comes to caring for patients, death is not failure. True failure is when clinicians are too afraid or too busy to acknowledge the reality of impending death, and patients are robbed of the opportunity to make sense of it.

Being Human: When Education Is Not Enough

The experience of death—just like loss and love and hope—is so deeply human and so emotionally complex that our rational minds struggle to take control when we are faced with it. As a result, the experience of death, and the aftermath for those who are left behind, can be complicated and confusing. It has certainly been that way for Shawn and me as we struggle to reconcile deeply conflicted feelings about the way my dad died.

Shawn has told me how it was much more difficult being a family member, in addition to being a doctor, when

Death is not failure.
True failure is when
clinicians are too
afraid or too busy to
acknowledge the
reality of impending
death, and patients
are robbed of the
opportunity to
make sense of it.

it came to talking to my dad about his goals and wishes for the end of his life. He has also told me how much easier it was to make hopeful assumptions about my dad's journey and overestimate how much time my dad had left. While physicians are notorious for overestimating survival, Shawn felt this to be particularly true when the person is also someone you love.[23] Needless to say, nearly the whole time my dad was sick, Shawn and I both convinced ourselves that despite everything we knew about terminal cancer, my dad's situation was different.

We regret that we didn't get to have important conversations with my dad about how he wanted the end to look, whether he felt prepared, whether he felt like he'd done and said the things he'd wanted to do and say before he left this earth. At the same time, my dad was someone who did not want to stop treatments and preferred to feel like he was "doing something" about his cancer, even if the treatments were making him sicker. And yet to complicate things further, he was specific about what that "doing something" looked like; he was unwilling to get a feeding tube when one of his doctors had suggested it, and he told us during his final hospital stay that he never wanted to be on a ventilator. "I don't ever want tubes going into me or coming out of me," he said. "I want to be me until the end."

Up until the time my dad died, he was receiving chemotherapy and therefore was unable (and perhaps unwilling) to enroll in hospice, even though he would have otherwise qualified. And though his symptoms were worsening, he had only met with members of his palliative care team a couple of times. It seemed to us that he associated palliative care with hospice care—and since he wasn't ready to enroll in hospice because he still wanted to pursue active treatment, he didn't engage much with his palliative team, even though he was able to receive palliative care alongside his cancer treatments. In my dad's mind, like so many other patients, it was all or nothing, one or the other. The artificial bifurcation of medicine into distinct "curative" and "palliative" spheres stopped my dad in his tracks and made him feel compelled to choose.

Because of all this, my dad didn't have many opportunities for conversations with his doctors about what he wanted when the end came. Shawn and I had talked to my dad on several occasions about goals for his care, but we knew we needed to have a more serious discussion, especially since my dad was physically declining rather rapidly, despite his optimism about his treatment plan. Although he had recently stayed in the ICU for a stomach bleed not long before he died, my dad seemed to be recovering and was preparing to start a new chemotherapy regimen the following week. So when he suddenly became short of breath and lost consciousness while Shawn and I were visiting him at his house, we were totally unprepared. We didn't think the end was so near for my dad, and our shared belief that he didn't "seem ready for hospice yet" undoubtedly contributed to the illusion that death was still far off for him.

Shawn and I have nearly twenty years of medical training and end-of-life research between the two of us. And yet when my dad began dying, our education meant nothing. Nothing could prepare us for that moment. We panicked. We called 911. And we did this despite the fact that everything we'd ever learned about end-of-life care told us that calling 911 would not be the best thing in the end.

Minutes later, an ambulance arrived. The scene became hectic quickly as the paramedics unloaded their truck, bringing a stretcher into my dad's house along with all the equipment necessary for resuscitation. My dad did not have an advanced directive, but he had clearly expressed to us that he did not want to spend any more time in hospitals and certainly did not want to be on a ventilator. So knowing his chances of survival were minimal and that even in the best-case scenario, he would likely end up intubated in the ICU, we asked the paramedics to not do the exact things they were trained to do. I pleaded with the lead paramedic to not start CPR before Shawn pulled him aside and asked him to call the emergency medicine physician at the hospital where they intended to bring my dad. Shawn asked the paramedic to explain to the doctor that my dad was terminally ill and his family was asking that he not be resuscitated given the irreversibility of his condition.

Fortunately the physician told the paramedic that it was OK to forgo resuscitation if that's what the family wanted. Seemingly relieved, the paramedics removed the oxygen mask from my dad's face and the electrodes from his abdomen. The team stayed with us for a while, helping to make sure that my dad was comfortable in his bed as his breaths became shallower and the pauses between them longer. Then they left us so that we could be alone with my dad in his final moments.

Just twenty minutes after the paramedics left, with his family, best friend, and pastor by his side, my dad took his last breath. The man who felt like such an unstoppable force was suddenly gone, and there was a gaping hole left in the world.

When I think about it, in many ways my dad did get to be himself in the end. He woke up that morning without any inclination that this particular day would be his last. He died believing he'd have more treatments and get more time. While Shawn and I still wish that the long path toward the end had looked differently for my dad, we also know that he died in a way that was not far from what he would have said he wanted, if he'd had the chance to say so.

What I've learned through all this is that dying is hard, and the difficulties we face at the end of life extend beyond the way medicine is practiced or how students are trained. Beneath the surface of medical education and practice lurks the undeniable reality that the issues surrounding death and dying are not simply systems issues; they are issues of body and soul, and they're woven within the human condition and inextricably bound up with our existential qualms about being mortal. While there exist real, system-wide barriers that prevent honest end-of-life conversations, recognizing these logistical barriers is not enough. All of us—patients, doctors, nurses, occupational and physical therapists, hospital executives, religious leaders, and lay people, rich and poor—need to dig deep and ask ourselves why we don't like to confront our mortality and why conversations about how we want to die don't happen often enough. We need to look where it hurts; we need to open the box that we slam shut and hold closed and face the things that frighten us the most. Ignoring the reality of death and burying our anxiety is helping no one. We cannot pretend that death is something that happens to others and never to us.

In her book *Cultivating Humanity*, philosopher Martha Nussbaum reminds us that "compassion requires a sense of our own vulnerability to misfortune." "To respond with compassion," she says, "I must be willing to entertain the thought that this suffering person might be me."[24] While we all are tempted to avoid negative emotion and minimize existential suffering, doing so gets in the way of our ability to connect with others when they need it most. It is precisely the ability to recognize that at any time, any one of us could get a terrible diagnosis or have a devastating

We cannot pretend that death is something that happens to others and never to us.

injury that moves us toward compassion. Acknowledging our shared mortality can help us better care for the people we love when they face the end before we do. When we do this, we begin to see the need to rally around them. We begin to see the need to be authentically present with them so that we can listen to them, ask them the questions that others might be too afraid to bring up, and begin to understand how they might want to live out the rest of their lives.

Had I known my mom would have felt such relief when she chose to "stop fighting" and begin hospice care, I would have listened more closely to what she wanted. Rather than being motivated by my own fear of losing her, I might have tried to hear her fears, hopes, and need for care and comfort when fighting became onerous and exhausting. And maybe I would have tried to initiate the conversations that I was so desperately trying to avoid. Like my mother, most patients don't need our exhortations to fight, our unrealistic promises of eventual healing, or our platitudes about things happening for a reason. What they need from us is honesty, vulnerability, and the courage to help them identify what matters most as the end draws near.

Undoubtedly, what they—all of us—also need are physicians and health care professionals who can imagine what it might be like to be a patient at the end of life and consider what they would want if they were facing death themselves. It's likely that they too would want honesty and compassion, that they would want a physician who was willing to come alongside them on their journey and help them navigate the uncertainty of it all. And maybe they'd even want someone willing to acknowledge the mortal wound we all share, someone who was willing to face the frailty of their own existence and confront the fact that they are subject to the indiscriminate throes of this universe as well. As nurse and ethicist Michele Carter says, "In the end, it is not death's dignity that will give our patients and us the peace we seek. It is the affirmation of who we are—moral, finite, vulnerable beings striving to fashion a life of our own."[25]

Affirming our shared mortality is the first step toward transforming the complicated relationship so many of us have with death and dying, both inside and outside medicine. But because so many of us receive care from and die within medical systems, we need to work toward creating clinical environments that account for the undeniably human elements of sickness, suffering, and care. We need to create spaces where students and clinicians can push against restrictive notions of objectivity and clinical distance—ideas that lead to compromised care for patients and moral distress for those who give that care. My medical students shouldn't feel that there is something wrong with them when they are shaken up by suffering and death; their performance on board exams shouldn't matter more than compassion and connection; and their success later as physicians shouldn't be determined strictly by output or efficiency. We should no longer tolerate a health care system that reduces the clinical encounter to a market exchange or tells clinicians and patients that fifteen minutes is enough time to care for someone. We should no longer accept a medical model that denies the human elements of illness and suffering that extend beyond the bounds of tests and metrics. We should no longer accept a medical culture that denies our need for others as we all attempt to make sense of death and loss.

In a system that causes so much suffering for both patients and clinicians, our connection to each other is our only way out.

We have found it impossible to talk about death and dying without talking about medicine. Over the past eighty years, the two have become utterly entwined in Western culture, particularly in the United States. Though death is a natural, inevitable, and deeply human process, it has fallen squarely within medicine's scope, despite the fact that few of us would describe medicine as "natural" or "deeply human." Medicine and medical training have, for the most part, been framed as technical endeavors focused on biological intervention. As a result, medicine more often (and more comfortably) intervenes physically in the care of those who are dying while neglecting the existential aspects that usually matter most.

While the hospice movement and development of palliative medicine have brought about invaluable changes in how we care for those who are suffering or dying, the problems with the way health care is delivered, practiced, and taught are so complex and pervasive that the introduction of hospice and palliative care has not been enough to change the larger culture of contemporary medicine. Until caring for human suffering that extends beyond the physical body is seen as part of the everyday practice of medicine, the existential—and sometimes even the biological—care of the dying will forever be seen as extraneous to the "real" work of medical care.

Perhaps nothing in contemporary medicine has brought the suffering of patients into sharper focus than the COVID-19 pandemic, which made landfall in the United States just after we finished the final draft of this book. Undoubtedly, countless volumes will be written about the ways the pandemic has changed the face of medicine, public health, politics, and our relationship to others. For now, however, we remain in its grip, and the true depth and breadth of the pandemic's lasting effects remain unclear. Yet, when it comes to end-of-life care, one thing is certain: COVID-19 has forced many of us to confront the questions we would rather put off, the very same existential questions medicine has avoided for so long.

Images of the disaster morgues and mass graves in New York City needed for the 22,000 bodies left in the wake of COVID-19 in a matter of two months are vivid glimpses into the sheer force of the pandemic's blow, a blow that the US health care system was not prepared to take. Suddenly, and horrifyingly, we all have been confronted with ethical issues we never anticipated: rationing limited resources like ventilators and ECMO machines, determining how much risk hospital workers should endure when supplies of personal protective equipment are low or totally depleted, and balancing the value of economic stability with that of human life. On top of this, inequality, inequity, and disparity have become even more glaring, as the most vulnerable among us—especially those who have been historically disenfranchised—experience disproportionate mortality rates, physical and emotional suffering, and economic hardship.

For us, it has been devastating to see so many people—even those without COVID-19—dying in hospitals alone, their loved ones unable to enter the building to be with them as they die. Shawn now finds himself calling husbands and wives, sons and daughters, to have some of the most difficult conversations about end-of-life decisions over the phone with people who will never see their loved ones awake, or perhaps even alive, ever again. We have watched as COVID-19 not only destroys human life but also eliminates the moments for connection and opportunities for compassion. We have watched it erase the time we want to be spending with those in our own lives whose time seems more limited than our own. In an effort to protect the most vulnerable, we stand by at a distance as our own grandparents live in relative isolation during what may be their last months with us.

What we cannot forget is that those spending their final days in isolation, those dying in staggering numbers in our ICUs, or those whose bodies are being processed in makeshift morgues each carry with them a story, stories filled with intense love, grief, disappointment, and joy. Their stories are unique and utterly individual, but for those who've died—or will die—within the walls of the hospital during this pandemic, their stories share a common and tragic ending: spending their final moments in the presence of strangers. Such tragedy is redeemed only by the fact that many of these strangers have shown unspeakable compassion in the middle of it all, finding time to be with patients as they die and bear witness to their final moments. We have heard stories, and have even seen firsthand, the love that health care workers have shown to patients as they take their final breaths, holding their hands, telling them they are safe, that they are not alone, that it is okay to let go of this life.

Yet, despite the love of these compassionate strangers, the consequences of isolation this pandemic has caused echo throughout the hospital. There are patients who receive unwanted care without their loved ones there to advocate for them, or those who lose heart in their loneliness, wishing for their end to come sooner—or those with COVID-19, dying in crowded isolation units who spend their final moments alone, in pain and fear and confusion. Watching this pandemic unfold has only intensified our belief that discussing, determining, and documenting our values and wishes for how we want to die is one of the most important things that any of us can do. We need a health care system that promotes this belief, one that encourages health care professionals to engage in these conversations before a crisis arrives and helps patients and their loved ones identify what would matter most to them if the end were to come sooner than they'd anticipated. Perhaps as we all experience the tragic losses that COVID-19 has brought with it, we will come closer to creating such a system. Perhaps all this loss presents us with an opportunity to recognize the importance of living and dying in a way that reflects who we are. Through this loss, we may begin to see those things that make life precious, and we might begin to ask ourselves what it will take to make our lives—and our deaths—more meaningful.

Medicine is replete with humanness; there are moments of healing, pain, loss, and love at nearly every turn. Changing the culture of medicine—particularly around death and dying—will require all of us to confront this humanness and walk right into it. Most of the time, what those who are dying need most from us is our presence—our willingness to come alongside them, listen to their hopes and fears, and help them know they are not alone. And this kind of presence can be healing for those who are dying as well as those who are there with them. If we are open to it, standing in the presence of suffering or loss can teach us what it means to show true compassion. These kinds of experiences, however, can be painful. Indeed, the word "compassion" quite literally means "the suffering of pain together."[1] Because of this, we need to ensure that we are also caring well for each other—and perhaps especially for those health professionals among us who spend

What those who are dying need most from us is our presence—our willingness to come alongside them, listen to their hopes and fears, to help them know they are not alone.

their days on the front lines of patient care. We must acknowledge that they too suffer in a system that denies the human experience of caring for others and minimizes the significance of death and dying.

Death is momentous. Its power reverberates throughout so many of our cultural, religious, and professional practices. To deny the existential gravity of death and loss is to deny one of the few things in this life we all share. Perhaps when we start to acknowledge the shared vulnerability of being mortal, we will begin to draw toward one another when we need it most.

Compassionate people are geniuses in the art of living, more necessary to the dignity, security, and joy of humanity than the discoverers of knowledge.

—Albert Einstein

ACKNOWLEDGMENTS

First and foremost, we must thank our families and closest friends. They've supported us through not only our training but also our experiences of death and loss, personally and professionally. Our life's work is rife with meaning, beauty, and pain, and we have so much gratitude to the people we love who choose to walk alongside us on our journeys. We know that the privilege we have to do this work—and write about it—is a result of the care and support we receive from all of you.

To our friends and colleagues who read, critiqued, and strengthened initial drafts of this book—Ned Stolzberg, Tom Fitch, Lisa Harrison, Sandra Miller, Rachele Piemonte, and Angela Thompson—thank you for taking time out of your busy lives to make such important contributions to this book. We want to especially thank our friend (and the best occupational therapist around) Charlie Wilson, who read every word of every draft. His invaluable feedback was matched only by his endless positivity and encouragement when we needed it most.

We are also grateful for the help and support we've received from the MIT Press team throughout this process, especially that of Phil Laughlin. Without Phil's generosity, insights, and encouragement, this book would not exist.

Finally, we want to thank our teachers: the mentors, students, and most especially patients who've guided and inspired us along the way—and who are the only reason we have anything to say at all.

Advance directive
Written statement of a person's wishes regarding medical treatment to ensure these wishes are carried out should the person become incapacitated. Often includes a living will and medical power of attorney.

Brain death
The Uniform Determination of Death Act (UDDA) asserts that "an individual who has sustained either (1) irreversible cessation of circulatory and respiratory functions, or (2) irreversible cessation of all functions of the entire brain, including the brain stem, is dead." All fifty US states have now adopted by law the neurological criteria for determining death (thirty-seven have adopted the UDDA word for word), recognizing the irreversible cessation of all functions of the entire brain as a valid criterion for death.

Concurrent care
Also referred to as open access or simultaneous care. Developed to remove financial and psychological barriers to hospice enrollment. In a concurrent care model, patients do not need to choose hospice, palliative care, and curative treatments in isolation and can receive curative treatment alongside hospice and palliative services.

Disability-adjusted life year (DALY)
Measurement indicating how many years of healthy life are lost to illness, disability, or premature death; one DALY can be thought of as one lost year of "healthy" life. The sum of these DALYs across a population measures the "disease burden" of a population, or the gap between current health and ideal health, where an entire population would live to an advanced age, free of disease and disability.

Do Not Intubate (DNI)
Medical orders indicating not to intubate a patient.

Do Not Resuscitate (DNR)
Medical orders indicating not to resuscitate a patient.

Electronic Health Record (EHR)
A digital version of a patient's paper chart or medical record.

Existential suffering
The ways in which patients suffer beyond their biological bodies—especially as they face serious, chronic, or terminal illnesses—including loss of meaning, identity, and previous ways of being in the world.

Fee for service
A reimbursement model in which a doctor or other health care professional is paid a fee for each particular service rendered (for example, tests, procedures, and office visits), incentivizing the volume and quantity of services.

Hospice care
Medical care that is usually reserved for those who have six months or fewer to live that addresses symptom management, coordination of care, communication and decision making, clarification of goals, and quality of life. Care is delivered by an interdisciplinary team that addresses physical, psychosocial, and spiritual/existential issues for both the person who is dying and their family.

Living will
Written statement detailing specific desires regarding medical treatment (for example, the use of a ventilator, certain medications, or feeding tubes) in circumstances in which patients are unable to speak for themselves.

Medical Assistance in Dying (MAiD)
Law passed in Canada in 2016 allowing an adult with decision-making capacity along with a "grievous and irremediable medical condition" to request aid in dying. In Canada, two types of MAiD are allowed: a physician or nurse practitioner can directly administer a medication that causes the death of the person who has requested it, or a physician or nurse practitioner can prescribe a medication that a person can administer themselves to cause their own death.

Medical power of attorney
A legal document that names a person who has the authority to make medical decisions on a patient's behalf should the patient become incapacitated.

Operative mortality
Any death, regardless of cause, occurring *within* thirty days after surgery (in or out of the hospital) or occurring *after* thirty days but during the same hospitalization subsequent to the operation.

Palliative care
Approach to care that emphasizes quality of life for patients who are facing serious or life-threatening illnesses through the prevention and relief of suffering, whether physical, psychosocial, or spiritual/existential. Palliative care can be offered at any stage of a serious illness and can be provided alongside curative treatments. It also includes care for patients' families.

Palliative medicine
A board-certified subspecialty of medicine in the United States since 2006. Physicians and health care professionals in the field of palliative medicine are trained to offer both hospice and palliative care to patients and their families.

Palliative sedation
Controlled and reversible process of using medication to reduce a patient's consciousness—sometimes to the point of total unconsciousness—to relieve severe, unremitting suffering for a patient who is terminally ill.

Physician aid in dying
Also known as physician-assisted death or aid in dying. A practice in the United States by which a physician provides a person who is deemed terminally ill with a prescription for a lethal dose of medication that the person intends to self-administer in order to cause death. Legal in ten US jurisdictions, physician aid in dying must be formally requested by a person who has been assessed for decision-making capacity and determined by two physicians to likely have six months or fewer to live.

Primary palliative care
Palliative care delivered by health care professionals who are *not* palliative care specialists, such as primary care clinicians; physicians in other medical specialties (such as cardiology and oncology); and nurses, social workers, pharmacists, chaplains, and others who care for patients with serious or life-threatening illness but are not certified in palliative care.

Specialized palliative care
Palliative care delivered by health care professionals who are specialists in the field, such as physicians board certified in palliative medicine as well as nurses, social workers, pharmacists, and chaplains certified in palliative care.

Total pain
As described by Dame Cicely Saunders, suffering that encompasses all of a person's physical, psychological, social, spiritual, and practical struggles.

Voluntary stopping of eating and drinking (VSED)
The conscious decision to refuse foods and fluids of any kind, including artificial nutrition and/or hydration, with the intention of hastening one's death.

Chapter 1

1. Nina R. O'Connor, Meredith Dougherty, Pamela S. Harris, and David J. Casarett, "Survival after Dialysis Discontinuation and Hospice Enrollment for ESRD," *Clinical Journal of the American Society of Nephrology: CJASN* 8, no. 12 (December 2013): 2117–2122.

2. Paul Komesaroff, "The Many Faces of the Clinic: A Levinasian View," in *Handbook of Phenomenology and Medicine*, ed. S. Kay Toombs (Dordrecht, Netherlands: Kluwer Academic Publishers, 2001), 317. The idea of the physician as detached observer of the body-object perpetuates an antiquated subject/object dualism.

3. Claudio Sandroni, Jerry Nolan, Fabio Cavallaro, and Massimo Antonelli, "In-Hospital Cardiac Arrest: Incidence, Prognosis, and Possible Measures to Improve Survival," *Intensive Care Medicine* 33, no. 2 (February 1, 2007): 237–245.

4. Sandroni et al., "In-Hospital Cardiac Arrest"; Renee D. Stapleton, William J. Ehlenbach, Richard A. Deyo, and J. Randall Curtis, "Long-Term Outcomes after In-Hospital CPR in Older Adults with Chronic Illness," *Chest* 146, no. 5 (November 2014): 1214–1225.

5. Gary M. Reisfield, Susannah Kish Wallace, Mark F. Munsell, Fern J. Webb, Edgar R. Alvarez, and George R. Wilson, "Survival in Cancer Patients Undergoing In-Hospital Cardiopulmonary Resuscitation: A Meta-Analysis," *Resuscitation* 71, no. 2 (November 1, 2006): 152–160.

6. Manish N. Shah, Rollin J. Fairbanks, and E. Brooke Lerner, "Cardiac Arrests in Skilled Nursing Facilities: Continuing Room for Improvement?," *Journal of the American Medical Directors Association* 8, no. 3 (March 1, 2007): e27–31.

7. Claas T. Buschmann and Michael Tsokos, "Frequent and Rare Complications of Resuscitation Attempts," *Intensive Care Medicine* 35, no. 3 (March 1, 2009): 397–404.

8. Romergryko G. Geocadin, Matthew A. Koenig, Xiaofeng Jia, Robert D. Stevens, and Mary Ann Peberdy, "Management of Brain Injury after Resuscitation from Cardiac Arrest," *Neurologic Clinics*, 26, no. 2 (May 1, 2008): 487–506.

9. Haresh L. Bhatia, Neal R. Patel, Neesha N. Choma, Jonathan Grande, Dario A. Giuse, and Christoph U. Lehmann, "Code Status and Resuscitation Options in the Electronic Health Record," *Resuscitation* 87 (February 2015): 14–20;

Daniela Lamas, Natalie Panariello, Natalie Henrich, Bernard Hammes, Laura C. Hanson, Diane E. Meier, Nancy Guinn, Janet Corrigan, Sean Hubber, Hannah Luetke-Stahlman, and Susan Block, "Advance Care Planning Documentation in Electronic Health Records: Current Challenges and Recommendations for Change," *Journal of Palliative Medicine* 21 (2018): 522–528.

10. Adina S. Weinerman, Irfan A. Dhalla, Alex Kiss, Edward E. Etchells, Robert C. Wu, and Brian M. Wong, "Frequency and Clinical Relevance of Inconsistent Code Status Documentation," *Journal of Hospital Medicine* 10, no. 8 (August 2015): 491–496.

11. Sarah Kliff, "Why American Medicine Still Runs on Fax Machines," *Vox*, October 30, 2017, accessed June 15, 2020, https://www.vox.com/health-care /2017/10/30/16228054/american-medical-system-fax-machines-why.

12. Maria J. Silveira, Scott Y. H. Kim, and Kenneth M. Langa, "Advance Directives and Outcomes of Surrogate Decision Making before Death," *New England Journal of Medicine* 362, no. 13 (April 1, 2010): 1211–1218.

13. Marc Tunzi, "Can the Patient Decide? Evaluating Patient Capacity in Practice," *American Family Physician* 64, no. 2 (July 15, 2001): 299; Barton W. Palmer and Alexandrea L. Harmell, "Assessment of Healthcare Decision-Making Capacity," *Archives of Clinical Neuropsychology* 31, no. 6 (September 2016): 530–540.

14. Sander M. Levin, "H.R.4449—101st Congress (1989–1990): Patient Self-Determination Act of 1990," July 2, 1990, accessed June 15, 2020, https:// www.congress.gov/bill/101st-congress/house-bill/4449.

15. Kuldeep N. Yadav, Nicole B. Gabler, Elizabeth Cooney, Saida Kent, Jennifer Kim, Nicole Herbst, Adjoa Mante, Scott D. Halpern, and Katherine R. Courtright, "Approximately One in Three US Adults Completes Any Type of Advance Directive for End-of-Life Care," *Health Affairs* 36, no. 7 (2017): 1244–1251.

16. Lamas et al., "Advance Care Planning."

17. Mohammadreza Hojat, Michael J. Vergare, Kaye Maxwell, George Brainard, Steven K. Herrine, Gerald A. Isenberg, Jon Veloski, and Joseph S. Gonnella, "The Devil Is in the Third Year: A Longitudinal Study of Erosion of Empathy in Medical School," *Academic Medicine* 84, no. 9 (September 2009): 1182–1191.

18. Atul Gawande, *Being Mortal: Medicine and What Matters in the End* (New York: Metropolitan Books, 2014); Paul Kalanithi, *When Breath Becomes Air* (New York: Random House Publishing Group, 2016); Jessica Nutik Zitter, *Extreme Measures: Finding a Better Path to the End of Life* (New York: Avery, 2017).

Chapter 2

1. Centers for Disease Control, "Data Table for Figure 30. Place of Death, by Age: United States, 2006, 2011, and 2016," accessed June 15, 2020, https://www.cdc.gov/nchs/data/hus/2017/fig30.pdf; "Exploring the Preferences for Place of Death among Cancer Patients and Their Family Caregiver," *Journal of Clinical Oncology*, October 10, 2015; California Healthcare Foundation, *Final Chapter: Californians' Attitudes and Experiences with Death and Dying*, February 2012, accessed June 15, 2020, https://www.chcf.org/wp-content/uploads/2017/12/PDF-FinalChapterDeathDying.pdf.

2. Charles E. Rosenberg, *The Care of Strangers: The Rise of America's Hospital System* (New York: Basic Books, 1987), 3–5.

3. Rosenberg, *The Care of Strangers*, 4; Paul Starr, *The Social Transformation of American Medicine* (New York: Basic, 1982), 149.

4. Starr, *The Social Transformation*, 149.

5. Philippe Ariès, *The Hour of Our Death: The Classic History of Western Attitudes toward Death over the Last One Thousand Years*, trans. Helen Weaver (New York: Alfred A. Knopf, 1981), 473, 559.

6. Ariès, *The Hour of Our Death*, 569.

7. Starr, *The Social Transformation*, 150–151.

8. Starr, *The Social Transformation*, 157, 154.

9. Rosenberg, *The Care of Strangers*, 134.

10. Rosenberg, *The Care of Strangers*, 141.

11. Rosenberg, *The Care of Strangers*, 150.

12. Starr, *The Social Transformation*, 145. New "cures" included a serum to treat diphtheria discovered by scientists in Berlin in 1891.

13. Rosenberg, *The Care of Strangers*, 8; Starr, *The Social Transformation*, 146.

14. Rosenberg, *The Care of Strangers*, 150 (emphasis added).

15. John Harley Warner, "The History of Science and the Sciences of Medicine," *Osiris*, 2nd series, vol. 10 (1995): 177.

16. Rosenberg, *The Care of Strangers*. See also Joel D. Howell, *Technology in the Hospital: Transforming Patient Care in the Early 20th Century* (Baltimore: Johns Hopkins University Press, 1996).

17. Rosenberg, *The Care of Strangers*, 9. See also Starr, *The Social Transformation*.

18. Rosenberg, *The Care of Strangers*, 10.

19. Vincent Mor, David S. Greer, and Robert Kastenbaum, "The Hospice Experiment: An Alternative in Terminal Care," in *The Hospice Experiment*, ed. Vincent Mor, David S. Greer, and Robert Kastenbaum (Baltimore: Johns Hopkins University Press, 1988), 3–4.

20. Frederick Adolf Paola, Robert Walker, and Lois LaCivita Nixon, *Medical Ethics and Humanities* (Sudbury, MA: Jones and Barlett Publishers, 2010), 386.

21. Starr, *The Social Transformation*, 336.

22. Paola, Walker, and Nixon, *Medical Ethics*, 386. See also David N. Oshinsky, *Polio: An American Story* (New York: Oxford University Press, 2005), 90.

23. Rosenberg, *The Care of Strangers*, 6.

24. Steven Laureys, Gastone G. Celesia, Francois Cohadon, Jan Lavrijsen, José León-Carrión, Walter G. Sannita, Leon Sazbon, et al., "Unresponsive Wakefulness Syndrome: A New Name for the Vegetative State or Apallic Syndrome," *BMC Medicine* 8 (November 2010): 68.

25. After a committee from Harvard Medical School offered a formal definition of brain death in 1968 and a report on brain death by the Task Force on Death and Dying appeared in 1972, a legal definition of brain death was published by a presidential commission in 1981 within the Uniform Determination of Death Act (UDDA). The UDDA, which is still used as model legislation for states today, asserts that "an individual who has sustained either (1) irreversible cessation of circulatory and respiratory functions, or (2) irreversible cessation of all functions of the entire brain, including the brain stem, is dead." All fifty states have now adopted by law the neurological criteria for determining death (thirty-seven have adopted the UDDA word for word), recognizing the irreversible cessation of all functions of the entire brain as a valid criterion for death. See Ad Hoc Committee of the Harvard Medical School to Examine the Definition of Brain Death, "A Definition of Irreversible Coma," *JAMA: Journal of the American Medical Association* 205, no. 6 (August 1968): 337–340; Task Force on Death and Dying of the Institute of Society, Ethics, and the Life Sciences, "Refinements in Criteria for the Determination of Death: An Appraisal," *JAMA: Journal of the American Medical Association* 221, no. 1 (July 1972): 48–53; President's Commission for the Study of Ethical Problems in Medicine and Biomedical and Behavioral Research, *Defining Death: Medical, Legal, and Ethical Issues in the Determination of Death*, 1981, accessed June 15, 2020, https:// repository.library.georgetown.edu/bitstream/handle/10822/559345/defining _death.pdf?sequence=1&isAllowed=y; Nikolas T. Nikas, Dorinda C. Bordlee, and Madeline Moreira, "Determination of Death and the Dead Donor Rule: A Survey of the Current Law on Brain Death," *Journal of Medicine and Philosophy* 41, no. 3 (2016): 237–256.

26. David Sudnow, *Passing On: The Social Organization of Dying* (Englewood Cliffs, NJ: Prentice Hall, 1967), 65.

27. David Wendell Moller, *On Death without Dignity: The Human Impact of Technological Dying* (Amityville, NY: Baywood, 1990), 58–59.

28. Thomas Cole and Nathan Carlin, "Faculty Health and the Crisis of Meaning: Humanistic Diagnosis and Treatment," in *Faculty Health in Academic Medicine: Physicians, Scientists, and the Pressures of Success*, ed. Thomas Cole, Thelma Jean Goodrich, and Ellen R. Gritz (Totowa, NJ: Humana Press, 2009), 148.

29. Sudnow, *Passing On*, 37.

30. Sudnow, *Passing On*, 74. Sudnow borrows this term from sociologist Erving Goffman.

31. Sudnow, *Passing On*, 71, 70.

32. Sudnow, *Passing On*, 44, 46.

33. Sudnow, *Passing On*, 71.

34. Barney G. Glaser and Anslem L. Strauss, *Awareness of Dying* (Chicago: Aldine, 1965), viii, vii, 3, 64.

35. David Field, "Palliative Medicine and the Medicalization of Death," *European Journal of Cancer Care* 94, no. 3 (1994): 60.

36. Glaser and Strauss, *Awareness of Dying*, 216.

Chapter 3

1. Philippe Ariès, *The Hour of Our Death: The Classic History of Western Attitudes toward Death over the Last One Thousand Years*, trans. Helen Weaver (New York: Alfred A. Knopf, 1981), 592.

2. Harold Y. Vanderpool, *Palliative Care: The 400-Year Quest for a Good Death* (Jefferson, NC: McFarland, 2015), 117.

3. Vanderpool, *Palliative Care*, 123.

4. Geoffrey Gorer, "The Pornography of Death," in *Death, Grief, and Mourning* (New York: Doubleday, 1955), 192–199.

5. Ariès, *The Hour of Our Death*, 582, 593.

6. Ariès, *The Hour of Our Death*, 560.

7. Vincent Mor, David S. Greer, and Robert Kastenbaum, "The Hospice Experiment: An Alternative in Terminal Care," in *The Hospice Experiment*, ed. Vincent Mor, David S. Greer, and Robert Kastenbaum (Baltimore: Johns Hopkins University Press, 1988), 7.

8. Elisabeth Kübler-Ross, *On Death and Dying* (New York: Macmillan, 1969), xi, 1, 9–10.

9. Mor, Greer, and Kastenbaum, "The Hospice Experiment," 8, 10.

10. Crossroads Hospice, "Remembering Dame Cicely Saunders: Founder of Hospice," accessed July 21, 2019, https://www.crossroadshospice.com/hospice-palliative-care-blog/2017/july/13/remembering-dame-cicely-saunders-founder-of-hospice/.

11. Caroline Richmond, "Dame Cicely Saunders, Founder of the Modern Hospice Movement, Dies," *BMJ: British Medical Journal* 327 (2005), accessed July 21, 2019, https://www.bmj.com/content/suppl/2005/07/18/331.7509.DC1.

12. Richmond, "Dame Cicely Saunders."

13. Crossroads Hospice, "Remembering Dame Cicely Saunders."

14. Dame Cicely Saunders, "Dying of Cancer," in *Cicely Saunders: Selected Writings, 1958–2004*, ed. Cicely Saunders and David Clark (New York: Oxford University Press, 2006), 11.

15. Mor, Greer, and Kastenbaum, "The Hospice Experiment," 11.

16. National Institute on Aging, "What Are Palliative Care and Hospice Care?," accessed July 21, 2019, https://www.nia.nih.gov/health/what-are-palliative-care-and-hospice-care.

17. National Institute on Aging, "What Are Palliative Care and Hospice Care?"

18. Mor, Greer, and Kastenbaum, "The Hospice Experiment," 9.

19. Sarah H. Cross and Haider J. Warraich, "Changes in the Place of Death in the United States," *New England Journal of Medicine* 381, no. 24 (December 12, 2019): 2369–2370.

20. Centers for Disease Control, "Data Table for Figure 30. Place of Death, by Age: United States, 2006, 2011, and 2016," accessed June 15, 2020, https://www.cdc.gov/nchs/data/hus/2017/fig30.pdf.

21. Jennifer S. Temel, Joseph A. Greer, Alona Muzikansky, Emily R. Gallagher, Sonal Admane, Vicki A. Jackson, Constance M. Dahlin, et al., "Early Palliative Care for Patients with Metastatic Non–Small-Cell Lung Cancer," *New England Journal of Medicine* 363, no. 8 (2010): 733–742; Stephen R. Connor, Bruce Pyenson, Kathryn Fitch, Carol Spence, and Kosuke Iwasaki, "Comparing Hospice and Nonhospice Patient Survival among Patients Who Die within a Three-Year Window," *Journal of Pain and Symptom Management* 33, no. 3 (2007): 238–246.

22. Diane E Meier, "Increased Access to Palliative Care and Hospice Services: Opportunities to Improve Value in Health Care," *The Milbank Quarterly* 89, no. 3 (September 2011): 343–380.

23. Meier, "Increased Access."

24. David Orentlicher, Thaddeus Mason Pope, and Ben A. Rich, "Clinical Criteria for Physician Aid in Dying," *Journal of Palliative Medicine* 19, no. 3 (2016): 259–262.

25. CNN, "Physician-Assisted Suicide Fast Facts," accessed August 12, 2019, https://www.cnn.com/2014/11/26/us/physician-assisted-suicide-fast-facts/index.html.

26. Orentlicher, Pope, and Rich, "Clinical Criteria."

27. American Medical Association, "Physician-Assisted Suicide," accessed March 5, 2020, https://www.ama-assn.org/delivering-care/ethics/physician -assisted-suicide; American Academy of Hospice and Palliative Medicine, "Physician-Assisted Dying," accessed March 5, 2020, http://aahpm.org/positions /pad.

28. American Academy of Hospice and Palliative Medicine, "Physician-Assisted Dying."

29. Roxanne Nelson, "Should Medical Aid in Dying Be Part of Hospice Care?," *Medscape*, February 26, 2020, accessed March 2, 2020, https://www.medscape .com/viewarticle/925769.

30. Nelson, "Should Medical Aid in Dying Be Part of Hospice Care?"

31. Government of Canada, Department of Justice, "Legislative Background: Medical Assistance in Dying," January 15, 2016, accessed February 23, 2020, https://www.justice.gc.ca/eng/rp-pr/other-autre/ad-am/p2.html.

32. Stefanie Green, *Medical Aid in Dying (MAiD)—Canada*, November 2019, accessed February 23, 2020, https://www.youtube.com/watch?v=4TJvR7Usu Xw&feature=youtu.be.

33. Green, *Medical Aid in Dying*.

34. Orentlicher, Pope, and Rich, "Clinical Criteria."

35. Eric L. Kraukauer, "Sedation at the End-of-Life," in *Oxford Textbook of Palliative Medicine*, ed. Nathan L. Cherry, Marie T. Fallon, Stein Kaasa, Russell K. Portenoy, and David C. Currow, 5th ed. (Oxford: Oxford University Press, 2015), 1134–1135.

36. Ahmed Elsayem, Eardie Curry III, Jeanette Boohene, Mark F. Munsell, Bianca Calderon, Frank Hung, and Eduardo Bruera, "Use of Palliative Sedation for Intractable Symptoms in the Palliative Care Unit of a Comprehensive Cancer Center," *Supportive Care in Cancer* 17, no. 1 (2009): 53–59.

37. Kraukauer, "Sedation at the End-of-Life," 1134.

38. Cynthia A. Meier and Thuan D. Ong, "To Feed or Not to Feed?: A Case Report and Ethical Analysis of Withholding Food and Drink in a Patient with Advanced Dementia," *Journal of Pain and Symptom Management* 50, no. 6 (December 1, 2015): 887–890.

Chapter 4

1. Emily Abel, "The Hospice Movement: Institutionalizing Innovation," *International Journal of Health Services* 18, no. 1 (1996): 81.

2. Atul Gawande, *Being Mortal: Medicine and What Matters in the End* (New York: Metropolitan Books, 2014), 5–6.

3. National Hospice and Palliative Care Organization, "Facts on Hospice and Palliative Care," 2017, accessed June 1, 2019, 4, https://www.nhpco.org/sites /default/files/public/Statistics_Research/2017_Facts_Figures.pdf.

4. Arizona Hospital and Healthcare Association, "End of Life Data," *Thoughtful Life Conversations*, 2018, accessed June 1, 2019, https://www.thoughtfullife conversations.org/end-of-life-care-data.

5. Erica R. Schockett, Joan M. Teno, Susan C. Miller, and Brad Stuart, "Late Referral to Hospice and Bereaved Family Member Perception of Quality of End-of-Life Care," *Journal of Pain and Symptom Management* 30, no. 5 (2005): 400–407.

6. Abel, "The Hospice Movement," 76.

7. United States Department of Health and Human Services, Office of Inspector General, "Hospices Inappropriately Billed Medicare Over $250 Million for General Inpatient Care," Daniel R. Levinson (Washington, DC: March 2016). https://oig.hhs.gov/oei/reports/oei-02-10-00491.pdf.

8. National Hospice and Palliative Care Organization, "Facts on Hospice," 4.

9. Jessica Rizzuto and Melissa D. Aldridge, "Racial Disparities in Hospice Outcomes: A Race or Hospice-Level Effect?," *Journal of the American Geriatrics Society* 66, no. 2 (2018): 407–413.

10. See, for example, Søren Kierkegaard, *Fear and Trembling and the Sickness unto Death*, trans. Walter Lowrie (Princeton, NJ: Princeton University Press, 1968); Martin Heidegger, *Being and Time* (New York: Harper Perennial Modern Classics, 2008); Kevin A. Aho, "Heidegger, Ontological Death, and the Healing Professions," *Medicine, Health Care, and Philosophy* 19, no. 1 (March 2016): 55–63; Nicole M. Piemonte, *Afflicted: How Vulnerability Can Heal Medical Education and Practice* (Cambridge, MA: MIT Press, 2018).

11. John F. Schumaker, William G. Warren, and Gary Groth-Marnat, "Death Anxiety in Japan and Australia," *Journal of Social Psychology* 131, no. 4 (August 1, 1991): 511–518; Jack F. Schumaker, Robert A. Barraclough, and Lisa M. Vagg, "Death Anxiety in Malaysian and Australian University Students," *Journal of Social Psychology* 128, no. 1 (February 1, 1988): 41–47.

12. Irvin D. Yalom, *Staring at the Sun: Overcoming the Terror of Death* (San Francisco: Jossey-Bass, 2009), 5.

13. Ernest Becker, *The Denial of Death* (New York: Free Press Paperbacks, 1997).

14. Sam Keen, foreword to *The Denial of Death*, by Ernest Becker (New York: Free Press Paperbacks, 1997), xii.

15. Jeffrey P. Bishop, *The Anticipatory Corpse: Medicine, Power, and the Care of the Dying* (Notre Dame, IN: University of Notre Dame Press, 2011), 17.

16. Sherwin B. Nuland, *How We Die: Reflections on Life's Final Chapter* (New York: Vintage Books, 1995), 258, 224.

17. Herman Feifel, "Death," in *Taboo Topics*, ed. Norman L. Farebrow (New York: Atherton Press, 1963), 11.

18. Herman Feifel, Susan Hanson, and Robert Jones, "Physicians Consider Death," *Proceedings of the 75th Annual Convention of the American Psychological Association* 2 (1967): 201–202. See also Anne C. Kane and John D. Hogan, "Death Anxiety in Physicians: Defensive Style, Medical Specialty, and Exposure to Death," *OMEGA: The Journal of Death and Dying* 16, no. 1 (January 1, 1985): 11–22.

19. See Douglas Black, Daniel Hardoff, and J. S. Nelki, "Educating Medical Students about Death and Dying," *Archives of Disease in Childhood* 64, no. 5 (May 1989): 750–753.

20. Aleksandra Ciałkowska-Rysz and Tomasz Dzierżanowski, "Personal Fear of Death Affects the Proper Process of Breaking Bad News," *Archives of Medical Science* 1 (2013): 127–131; Scott A. Fields and W. Michael Johnson, "Physician-Patient Communication: Breaking Bad News," *West Virginia Medical Journal* 108, no. 2 (2011): 32–35; Feifel, "Death," 10; Elisabeth Kübler-Ross, *On Death and Dying* (New York: Macmillan, 1969).

21. Sandra Kocijan Lovko, Rudolf Gregurek, and Dalibor Karlovic, "Stress and Ego-Defense Mechanisms in Medical Staff at Oncology and Physical Medicine Departments," *European Journal of Psychiatry* 21, no. 4 (December 2007): 279–286.

22. Peter Maguire, "Barriers to Psychological Care of the Dying," *British Medical Journal (Clinical Research Ed.)* 291, no. 6510 (December 14, 1985): 1712.

23. Piemonte, *Afflicted*.

24. Jeffrey Phillip Jacobs, Constantine Mavroudis, Marshall Lewis Jacobs, Bohdan Maruszewski, Christo I. Tchervenkov, François G. Lacour-Gayet, David Robinson Clarke, et al., "What Is Operative Mortality?: Defining Death in a Surgical Registry Database: A Report of the STS Congenital Database Taskforce and the Joint EACTS-STS Congenital Database Committee," *Annals of Thoracic Surgery* 81, no. 5 (May 2006): 1937–1941.

25. Caroline Chen, "Feds to Investigate Hospital Alleged to Have Kept Vegetative Patient Alive to Game Transplant Survival Rates," *ProPublica*, October 8, 2019, accessed March 1, 2020, https://www.propublica.org/article/feds -to-investigate-hospital-alleged-to-have-kept-vegetative-patient-alive-to-game -transplant-survival-rates.

26. Caroline Chen, "'It's Very Unethical': Audio Shows Hospital Kept Vegetative Patient on Life Support to Boost Survival Rates," October 3, 2019, accessed

March 1, 2020, https://www.propublica.org/article/audio-shows-hospital-kept -vegetative-patient-on-life-support-to-boost-survival-rates.

27. Karen Steinhauser, Nicholas A. Christakis, Elizabeth C. Clipp, Maya Mc-Neilly, Steven Grambow, Joanna Parker, and James A. Tulsky, "Preparing for the End of Life: Preferences of Patients, Families, Physicians, and Other Care Providers," *Journal of Pain and Symptom Management* 22, no. 3 (2001): 728.

28. Institute of Medicine, *Dying in America: Improving Quality and Honoring Individual Preferences Near the End of Life* (Washington, DC: National Academies Press, 2015), accessed March 15, 2020, https://www.nap.edu/read/18748 /chapter/1#ii. See also Betty R. Ferrell, Martha L. Twaddle, Amy Melnick, and Diane E. Meier, "National Consensus Project Clinical Practice Guidelines for Quality Palliative Care Guidelines, 4th Edition," *Journal of Palliative Medicine*, September 4, 2018 (emphasis added).

29. Bishop, *The Anticipatory Corpse*, 283.

30. Bishop, *The Anticipatory Corpse*, 257.

31. Bethne Hart, Peter Sainsbury, and Stephanie Short, "Whose Dying?: A Sociological Critique of the 'Good Death,'" *Mortality* 3, no. 1 (1998): 65, 72.

32. Sandra M. Gilbert, *Death's Door: Modern Dying and the Ways We Grieve* (New York: W. W. Norton and Company, 2006), 200–201.

33. Karen E. Steinhauser and James A. Tulsky, "Defining a 'Good' Death," in *Oxford Textbook of Palliative Medicine*, ed. Nathan L. Cherry, Marie T. Fallon, Stein Kaasa, Russell K. Portenoy, and David C. Currow, 5th ed. (Oxford: Oxford University Press, 2015), 81.

34. LaVera Crawley and Jonathan Koffman, "Ethnic and Cultural Aspects of Palliative Care," in *Oxford Textbook of Palliative Medicine*, Nathan L. Cherry, Marie T. Fallon, Stein Kaasa, Russell K. Portenoy, and David C. Currow, 5th ed. (Oxford: Oxford University Press, 2015).

35. Ariès, *The Hour of Our Death*, 586.

36. Ariès, *The Hour of Our Death*, 570–571.

37. Arizona Hospital and Healthcare Association, "End of Life Data."

38. Kaiser Family Foundation, "Public Strongly Favors End-of-Life Conversations between Doctors and Patients, with about Eight in 10 Saying Medicare and Other Insurers Should Cover These Visits," September 30, 2015, accessed January 18, 2020, https://www.kff.org/health-costs/press-release /public-strongly-favors-end-of-life-conversations-between-doctors-and-patients -with-about-eight-in-10-saying-medicare-and-other-insurers-should-cover-these -visits/.

39. John W. Lannamann, Linda M. Harris, Alexis D. Bakos, and Kylene J. Baker, "Ending the End-of-Life Communication Impasse," in *Cancer, Communication,*

and Aging, ed. Lisa H. Sparks, Dan O'Hair, and Gary L. Kreps (Cresskill, NJ: Hampton, 2008), 293–318.

40. Richard P. McQuellon and Michael A. Cowan, "Turning toward Death Together: Conversation in Mortal Time," *American Journal of Hospice and Palliative Medicine* 17, no. 5 (September 1, 2000): 315.

41. Casey Sharpe, "Toward an Experiential Definition of Palliative Care" (unpublished manuscript under review with *Journal of Pain and Symptom Management*).

42. Sharpe, "Toward an Experiential Definition of Palliative Care."

Chapter 5

1. Centers for Medicare and Medicaid Services, "National Health Expenditure Data: Historical," accessed March 10, 2020, https://www.cms.gov /Research-Statistics-Data-and-Systems/Statistics-Trends-and-Reports/National HealthExpendData/NationalHealthAccountsHistorical.

2. Shenggen Fan, "The Multibillion Dollar Question: How Much Will It Cost to End Hunger and Undernutrition?," Thomson Reuters Foundation, March 14, 2018, accessed June 17, 2020, https://reliefweb.int/report/world/multibillion -dollar-question-how-much-will-it-cost-end-hunger-and-undernutrition.

3. Preamble to the Constitution of World Health Organization as adopted by the International Health Conference, New York, June 19–July 22, 1946; signed on July 22, 1946, by the representatives of sixty-one states (Official Records of WHO, no. 2, 100), and entered into force on April 7, 1948.

4. America's Health Rankings, "Findings, International Comparison, 2018 Annual Report," accessed March 10, 2020, https://www.americashealthrankings .org/learn/reports/2018-annual-report/findings-international-comparison.

5. World Health Organization, "WHO Metrics: Disability-Adjusted Life Year (DALY)," Peterson-Kaiser Health System Tracker, 2020, accessed March 28, 2020, https://www.who.int/healthinfo/global_burden_disease/metrics_daly /en/.

6. Institute for Health Metrics and Evaluation, "GBD Data," April 18, 2014, accessed March 10, 2020, http://www.healthdata.org/gbd/data; Bradley Sawyer and Daniel McDermott, "How Does the Quality of the U.S. Healthcare System Compare to Other Countries?," March 28, 2019, accessed June 17, 2020, https://www.healthsystemtracker.org/chart-collection/quality-u-s -healthcare-system-compare-countries/.

7. Sawyer and McDermott, "How Does the Quality of the U.S. Healthcare System Compare to Other Countries?"

8. Sawyer and McDermott, "How Does the Quality of the U.S. Healthcare System Compare to Other Countries?"

9. Roosa Tikkanen and Melinda K. Abrams, "U.S. Health Care from a Global Perspective, 2019: Higher Spending, Worse Outcomes?," Commonwealth Fund, January 30, 2020, accessed March 1, 2020, https://www.common wealthfund.org/publications/issue-briefs/2020/jan/us-health-care-global -perspective-2019.

10. M. S. Reddy and Starlin Vijay Mythri, "Health-Care Ethics and the Free Market Value System," *Indian Journal of Psychological Medicine* 38, no. 5 (2016): 371–375.

11. John C. Goodman, "Why Not Try Free Market Health Care?," *Forbes*, October 17, 2019, accessed March 28, 2020, https://www.forbes.com/sites /johngoodman/2019/10/17/why-not-try-free-market-health-care/.

12. Robert J. Shiller, "Faith in an Unregulated Free Market?: Don't Fall for It," *New York Times*, October 9, 2015, accessed March 15, 2020, https://www .nytimes.com/2015/10/11/upshot/faith-in-an-unregulated-free-market-dont -fall-for-it.html.

13. David Belk and Paul Belk, "The Pharmaceutical Industry," *True Cost of Healthcare*, accessed March 22, 2020, http://truecostofhealthcare.org/the _pharmaceutical_industry/.

14. Belk and Belk, "The Pharmaceutical Industry."

15. National Association of Insurance Commissioners, "U.S. Health Insurance Industry, 2018, Annual Results," 2018, accessed March 22, 2020, https://naic .org/documents/topic_insurance_industry_snapshots_2018_health_ins_ind _report.pdf.

16. Emily Gee, "The High Price of Hospital Care," Center for American Progress, June 26, 2019, accessed March 22, 2020, https://www.americanprogress.org /issues/healthcare/reports/2019/06/26/471464/high-price-hospital-care/. See also Andrea M. Sisko, Sean P. Keehan, John A. Poisal, Gigi A. Cuckler, Sheila D. Smith, Andrew J. Madison, Kathryn E. Rennie, and James C. Hardesty, "National Health Expenditure Projections, 2018–27: Economic and Demographic Trends Drive Spending and Enrollment Growth," *Health Affairs* 38, no. 3 (February 2019): 491–501.

17. Institute of Medicine, *Best Care at Lower Cost: The Path to Continuously Learning Healthcare in America* (Washington, DC: National Academies Press, 2013).

18. Michelle M. Mello, Amitabh Chandra, Atul A. Gawande, and David M. Studdert, "National Costs of the Medical Liability System," *Health Affairs* 29, no. 9 (September 1, 2010): 1569–1577.

19. Alexi A. Wright and Ingrid T. Katz, "Beyond Burnout—Redesigning Care to Restore Meaning and Sanity for Physicians," *New England Journal of Medicine* 378, no. 4 (January 25, 2018): 309–311; Christine Sinsky, Lacey Colligan, Ling Li, Mirela Prgomet, Sam Reynolds, Lindsey Goeders, Johanna Westbrook, et al., "Allocation of Physician Time in Ambulatory Practice: A Time and Motion Study in 4 Specialties," *Annals of Internal Medicine* 165, no. 11 (December 6, 2016): 753.

20. Maria Panagioti, Efharis Panagopoulou, Peter Bower, George Lewith, Evangelos Kontopantelis, Carolyn Chew-Graham, Shoba Dawson, et al., "Controlled Interventions to Reduce Burnout in Physicians: A Systematic Review and Meta-analysis," *JAMA Internal Medicine* 177 (2017): 195–205.

21. David U. Himmelstein, Terry Campbell, and Steffie Woolhandler, "Health Care Administrative Costs in the United States and Canada, 2017," *Annals of Internal Medicine* 172, no. 2 (January 21, 2020): 134–142.

22. Abigail Abrams, "The U.S. Spends $2,500 per Person on Health Care Administrative Costs, Canada Spends $550. Here's Why," *TIME*, January 6, 2020, accessed March 29, 2020, https://time.com/5759972/health-care -administrative-costs/.

23. Abrams, "The U.S. Spends $2,500."

24. Kriti Prasad, Sara Poplau, Roger Brown, Steven Yale, Ellie Grossman, Anita B. Varkey, Eric Williams, et al., "Time Pressure during Primary Care Office Visits: A Prospective Evaluation of Data from the Healthy Work Place Study," *Journal of General Internal Medicine* 35, no. 2 (February 1, 2020): 465–472; M. Kim Marvel, Ronald M. Epstein, Kristine Flowers, and Howard B. Beckman, "Soliciting the Patient's Agenda: Have We Improved?." *JAMA* 281, no. 3 (January 20, 1999): 283–287; Donna R. Rhoades, Kay F. McFarland, W. H. Finch, and Andrew O. Johnson, "Speaking and Interruptions during Primary Care Office Visits," *Family Medicine* 33, no. 7 (August 2001): 528–532; Estella M. Geraghty, Peter Franks, and Richard L. Kravitz, "Primary Care Visit Length, Quality, and Satisfaction for Standardized Patients with Depression," *Journal of General Internal Medicine* 22, no. 12 (December 2007): 1641–1647.

25. UnitedHealth Group, "The High Cost of Avoidable Hospital Emergency Department Visits," July 22, 2019, accessed March 29, 2020, https://www .unitedhealthgroup.com/newsroom/posts/2019-07-22-high-cost-emergency -department-visits.html.

26. T. R. Reid, "How We Spend $3,400,000,000,000," *Atlantic*, June 15, 2017, accessed March 20, 2020, https://www.theatlantic.com/health/archive/2017 /06/how-we-spend-3400000000000/530355/.

27. Arizona Hospital and Healthcare Association, "End of Life Data," 2018, accessed June 1, 2019, https://static1.squarespace.com/static/57684fb7579 fb3ab7145720c/t/5bcf2934f9619a0ebc0df06c/1540303166635/EOL+Data +2018.pdf.

28. Robert Twycross, "A Tribute to Dame Cicely Saunders," St. Christopher's Hospice, accessed March 29, 2020, https://www.stchristophers.org.uk/about /damecicelysaunders/tributes.

29. Sean R. Morrison, Joan D. Penrod, J. Brian Cassel, Melissa Caust-Ellenbogen, Ann Litke, Lynn Spragens, and Diane E. Meier, "Cost Savings Associated with US Hospital Palliative Care Consultation Programs," *Archives of Internal Medicine* 168, no. 16 (September 8, 2008): 1783–1790; Ezekiel J. Emanuel, "Cost Savings at the End of Life: What Do the Data Show?," *JAMA: Journal of the American Medical Association* 275, no. 24 (June 26, 1996): 1907–1914.

30. Sean R. Morrison, Jessica Dietrich, Susan Ladwig, Timothy Quill, Joseph Sacco, John Tangeman, and Diane E. Meier, "Palliative Care Consultation Teams Cut Hospital Costs for Medicaid Beneficiaries," *Health Affairs* 30, no. 3 (March 1, 2011): 454–463; Joan D. Penrod, Partha Deb, Cornelia Dellenbaugh, James F. Burgess Jr., Carolyn W. Zhu, Cindy L. Christiansen, Carol A. Luhrs, et al., "Hospital-Based Palliative Care Consultation: Effects on Hospital Cost," *Journal of Palliative Medicine* 13, no. 8 (August 2010): 973–979.

31. Melissa D. Aldridge and Amy S. Kelley, "The Myth regarding the High Cost of End-of-Life Care," *American Journal of Public Health* 105, no. 12 (December 2015): 2411–2415.

32. Ezekiel J. Emanuel and Linda L. Emanuel, "The Economics of Dying—The Illusion of Cost Savings at the End of Life," *New England Journal of Medicine* 330, no. 8 (February 24, 1994): 540–544.

33. David J. Casarett, Jessica M. Fishman, Hien L. Lu, Peter J. O'Dwyer, Frances K. Barg, Mary D. Naylor, and David A. Asch, "The Terrible Choice: Re-Evaluating Hospice Eligibility Criteria for Cancer," *Journal of Clinical Oncology* 27, no. 6 (February 20, 2009): 953–959.

34. Casarett et al., "The Terrible Choice."

35. Casarett et al., "The Terrible Choice."

36. Vincent Mor, Todd H. Wagner, Cari Levy, Mary Ersek, Susan C. Miller, Risha Gidwani-Marszowski, Nina Joyce, et al., "Association of Expanded VA Hospice Care with Aggressive Care and Cost for Veterans with Advanced Lung Cancer," *JAMA Oncology* 5, no. 6 (June 1, 2019): 810–816.

37. Alena Baquet-Simpson, Claire M. Spettell, Allison N. Freeman, Angelina M. Bates, Harold L. Paz, Robert Mirsky, Daniel B. Knecht, et al., "Aetna's

Compassionate Care Program: Sustained Value for Our Members with Advanced Illness," *Journal of Palliative Medicine* 22, no. 11 (June 10, 2019): 1324–1330.

38. Krista L. Harrison and Stephen R. Connor, "First Medicare Demonstration of Concurrent Provision of Curative and Hospice Services for End-of-Life Care," *American Journal of Public Health* 106, no. 8 (August 2016): 1405–1408.

39. Ashish K. Jha, "End-of-Life Care, Not End-of-Life Spending," *News@JAMA* (blog), July 13, 2018, accessed March 25, 2020, https://newsatjama.jama .com/2018/07/13/jama-forum-end-of-life-care-not-end-of-life-spending/.

40. Baohui Zhang, Alexi A. Wright, Haiden A. Huskamp, Matthew E. Nilsson, Matthew L. Maciejewski, Craig C. Earle, Susan D. Block, et al., "Health Care Costs in the Last Week of Life: Associations with End of Life Conversations," *Archives of Internal Medicine* 169, no. 5 (March 9, 2009): 480–488.

41. Atul Gawande, *Being Mortal: Medicine and What Matters in the End* (New York: Metropolitan Books, 2014), 233, 234.

Chapter 6

1. Irvin D. Yalom, *Staring at the Sun: Overcoming the Terror of Death* (San Francisco: Jossey-Bass, 2009), 5.

2. Nicole M. Piemonte, *Afflicted: How Vulnerability Can Heal Medical Education and Practice* (Cambridge, MA: MIT Press, 2018). See also Kevin A. Aho, "Heidegger, Ontological Death, and the Healing Professions," *Medicine, Health Care, and Philosophy* 19, no. 1 (March 2016): 55–63.

3. Kathryn Montgomery, *How Doctors Think: Clinical Judgment and the Practice of Medicine* (New York: Oxford University Press, 2005), 36.

4. Lorraine Daston and Peter Galison, *Objectivity* (New York: Zone Books, 2007).

5. Ronald A. Carson, "The Hyphenated Space: Liminality in the Doctor-Patient Relationship," in *Stories Matter: The Role of Narrative in Medical Ethics*, ed. Rita Charon and Martha Montello (New York: Routledge, 2002), 180.

6. Diane E. Meier, "'I Don't Want Jenny to Think I'm Abandoning Her': Views on Overtreatment," *Health Affairs* 33, no. 5 (2014): 895–898.

7. Barbara A. Head, Tara J. Schapmire, Lori Earnshaw, John Chenault, Mark Pfeifer, Susan Sawning, and Monica A. Shaw, "Improving Medical Graduates' Training in Palliative Care: Advancing Education and Practice," *Advances in Medical Education and Practice* 7 (February 2016): 99–113. See also Amy Paturel, "Let's Talk about Death," Association of American Medical Colleges, January 15, 2019, accessed August 1, 2019, https://news.aamc.org/medical-education /article/lets-talk-about-death/.

8. Head et al., "Improving Medical Graduates' Training."

9. Christine Cowgill, "Urgent Need for Better End-of-Life Training," *Today's Geriatric Medicine*, accessed August 1, 2019, http://www.todaysgeriatricmedicine.com/news/ex_062613.shtml.

10. Edward H. Liston, "Education on Death and Dying: A Neglected Area in the Medical Curriculum," *Omega: Journal of Death and Dying* 6, no. 3 (1975): 193–198.

11. Harold Y. Vanderpool, *Palliative Care: The 400-Year Quest for a Good Death* (Jefferson, NC: McFarland, 2015), 126.

12. Head et al., "Improving Medical Graduates' Training," 111.

13. Head et al., "Improving Medical Graduates' Training."

14. Jessica M. Schmit, Lynne E. Meyer, Jennifer M. Duff, Yunfeng Dai, Fei Zou, and Julia L. Close, "Perspectives on Death and Dying: A Study of Resident Comfort with End-of-Life Care," *BMC Medical Education* 16, no. 297 (2016): 1–6.

15. Jane Gibbins, Rachel McCoubrie, and Karen Forbes, "Why Are Newly Qualified Doctors Unprepared to Care for Patients at the End of Life?," *Medical Education* 45, no. 4 (April 2011): 398, 393, 394, 396.

16. Paturel, "Let's Talk about Death."

17. Barbara A. Head, Lori A. Earnshaw, Ruth B. Greenberg, Robert C. Morehead, Mark P. Pfeifer, and Monica Ann Shaw, "'I Will Never Forget': What We Learned from Medical Student Reflections on a Palliative Care Experience," *Journal of Palliative Medicine* 15, no. 5 (May 2012): 535, 537, 539, 538.

18. Cynthia M. Williams, Cindy C. Wilson, and Cara H. Olsen, "Dying, Death, and Medical Education: Student Voices," *Journal of Palliative Medicine* 8, no. 2 (April 2005): 372–381.

19. Montgomery, *How Doctors Think*.

20. Medicare Program; Revisions to Payment Policies under the Physician Fee Schedule and Other Revisions to Part B for CY 2016; Final Rule, *Federal Register* 80, no. 220 (2015): 70886–71386, accessed January 19, 2020, https://www.gpo.gov/fdsys/pkg/FR-2015-11-16/pdf/2015-28005.pdf.

21. Meier, "'I Don't Want Jenny to Think I'm Abandoning Her,'" 897.

22. Paul Kalanithi, *When Breath Becomes Air* (New York: Random House, 2016), 166.

23. Paul Glare, Kiran Virik, Mark Jones, Malcolm Hudson, Steffen Eychmuller, John Simes, and Nicholas Christakis, "A Systematic Review of Physicians' Survival Predictions in Terminally-Ill Cancer Patients," *BMJ: British Medical Journal* 327, no. 7408 (July 26, 2003): 195–198; Nicholas A. Christakis and Elizabeth B. Lamont, "Extent and Determinants of Error in Physicians'

Prognoses in Terminally Ill Patients," *Western Journal of Medicine* 172, no. 5 (May 2000): 310–313.

24. Martha C. Nussbaum, *Cultivating Humanity: A Classical Defense of Reform in Liberal Education* (Cambridge, MA: Harvard University Press, 1998), 91.

25. Michele A. Carter, "Abiding Loneliness: An Existential Perspective on Loneliness," *Second Opinion* 3 (2000): 50.

Epilogue

1. The etymology of compassion is from the Latin *passion*, meaning the suffering of pain and *com*, meaning in combination or union together.

FURTHER READING

Aho, Kevin, ed. *Existential Medicine: Essays on Health and Illness*. Lanham, MD: Rowman and Littlefield International, 2018.

Ariès, Philippe. *The Hour of Our Death: The Classic History of Western Attitudes toward Death over the Last One Thousand Years*. Translated by Helen Weaver. New York: Alfred A. Knopf, 1981.

Becker, Ernest. *The Denial of Death*. New York: Free Press Paperbacks, 1997.

Bishop, Jeffrey P. *The Anticipatory Corpse: Medicine, Power, and the Care of the Dying*. Notre Dame, IN: University of Notre Dame Press, 2011.

Carter, Michele A. "Abiding Loneliness: An Existential Perspective on Loneliness." *Second Opinion* 3 (2000): 50.

Frankl, Viktor E. *Man's Search for Meaning*. Boston: Beacon Press, 2006.

Gawande, Atul. *Being Mortal: Medicine and What Matters in the End*. New York: Metropolitan Books, 2014.

Head, Barbara A., Lori A. Earnshaw, Ruth B. Greenberg, Robert C. Morehead, Mark P. Pfeifer, and Monica Ann Shaw. "'I Will Never Forget': What We Learned from Medical Student Reflections on a Palliative Care Experience." *Journal of Palliative Medicine* 15, no. 5 (May 2012): 535–541.

Kalanithi, Paul. *When Breath Becomes Air*. New York: Random House Publishing Group, 2016.

Kaufman, Sharon R. *And a Time to Die: How American Hospitals Shape the End of Life*. Chicago: University of Chicago Press, 2006.

Kübler-Ross, Elisabeth. *On Death and Dying*. New York: Macmillan, 1969.

McQuellon, Richard P., and Michael A. Cowan. "Turning toward Death Together: Conversation in Mortal Time." *American Journal of Hospice and Palliative Medicine* 17, no. 5 (September 1, 2000): 312–318.

Meier, Diane E. "'I Don't Want Jenny to Think I'm Abandoning Her': Views on Overtreatment." *Health Affairs* 33, no. 5 (2014): 895–898.

Miller, B. J., and Shoshana Berger. *A Beginner's Guide to the End: Practical Advice for Living Life and Facing Death*. New York: Simon and Schuster, 2019.

Montgomery, Kathryn. *How Doctors Think: Clinical Judgment and the Practice of Medicine*. New York: Oxford University Press, 2005.

Nuland, Sherwin B. *How We Die: Reflections on Life's Final Chapter*. New York: Vintage Books, 1995.

Piemonte, Nicole M. *Afflicted: How Vulnerability Can Heal Medical Education and Practice*. Cambridge, MA: MIT Press, 2018.

Quill, Timothy E., and Amy P. Abernethy. "Generalist plus Specialist Palliative Care—Creating a More Sustainable Model." *New England Journal of Medicine* 368, no. 13 (2013): 1173–1175.

Saunders, Cicely. "The Evolution of Palliative Care." *Patient Education and Counseling* 41, no. 1 (2000): 7–13.

Vanderpool, Harold Y. *Palliative Care: The 400-Year Quest for a Good Death*. Jefferson, NC: McFarland, 2015.

Zitter, Jessica Nutik. *Extreme Measures: Finding a Better Path to the End of Life*. New York: Avery, 2017.

INDEX

and mainstream medicine, 24,
157, 161, 188
medical denial of, 188–190
Suicide, 122
Surgery, 43, 124
Surrogate decision makers, 18–19
Survival rates, 11, 95–96
Sweden, 121

Tasma, David, 58
Technology, medical, 44, 46
Terminal illness, 50–51, 79, 88–89
Total pain, 72–74. *See also* Suffering
Transplants, 96–97
Treatment, conversations about,
26–28, 77
Tufts University School of Medicine,
168

United Kingdom, 58
United States
aid in dying, 64–66, 69–70
DALY rates, 121
end-of-life expenses, 141–142
health care spending, 119, 130
home/hospice deaths, 63
hospice care in, 60–61
hospital profits, 126–127
life expectancy, 120–121
mortality rates, 121
suicide rate, 122
University of California, 168
University of Louisville, 168

Ventilators, 46
Veterans Affairs (VA), Department
of, 145
Voluntarily stop eating and drinking
(VSED), 71–72

Vulnerability, 171–172

When Breath Becomes Air, 175
Wishes of patients, 16–22, 107–109,
186–187, 192–193. *See also* End-
of-life conversations
Wright, Alexi, 129

Yalom, Irvin, 89–90, 155

Zatulovsky, Yelena, 66

The MIT Press Essential Knowledge Series

NICOLE PIEMONTE, PHD, is the assistant dean for medical education and an assistant professor in the Department of Medical Humanities at Creighton University School of Medicine, Phoenix Regional Campus in Arizona. She received her PhD in medical humanities from The University of Texas Medical Branch, where she studied continental philosophy, medical ethics, literature and medicine, and medical epistemology. She is the author of *Afflicted: How Vulnerability Can Heal Medical Education and Practice* (MIT Press, 2018).

SHAWN ABREU, MD, practices hospice and palliative medicine and serves as a medical director at Hospice of the Valley in Phoenix, Arizona, where he cares for patients and teaches medical students, residents, and fellows. He received his medical degree from The University of Texas Medical Branch before completing his residency training in family medicine at the University of Arizona College of Medicine Phoenix, and then his fellowship training in hospice and palliative medicine at the Mayo Clinic in Arizona.